christine thomas

it doesn't have to be like this

to be like this

women and the struggle for socialism

christine thomas

it doesn't have to be like this
women and the struggle for socialism

Published by Socialist Publications Ltd

August 2010

It doesn't have to be like this
Women and the struggle for socialism
Christine Thomas
© Socialist Publications, 2010

First Edition August 2010

ISBN: 978-1-870958-39-4

Published by Socialist Publications
www.socialistparty.org.uk
Typeset in Utopia 9 pt
Printed by Russell Press (Nottingham)

Distribution by Socialist Books,
PO Box 24697, London, E11 1YD
Telephone +44 (0)20 8988 8789
e-mail: bookshop@socialistparty.org.uk
www.socialistbooks.co.uk

typesetting & design: dennis@kavitagraphics.co.uk

christine thomas

it doesn't have to be like this
women and the struggle for socialism

IT DOESN'T HAVE TO BE LIKE THIS

Introduction

A t the turn of the millennium we were promised that women's equality was just around the corner – and to many it really did seem possible. We had travelled such a long way compared to our grandparents and even our parents' generations. Legally women had the same rights as men, girls were outperforming boys in school and the labour market was so transformed that in some countries women had become a majority of the workforce. Economic and social changes were undermining traditional ideas about men and women's roles in society and significantly altering personal relations.

But scratch the surface and the old inequalities and discrimination had not disappeared. Despite laws against inequality, women's wages in the more economically developed countries were still on average much lower than those of men. So most women continued to shoulder the main responsibility for childcare and housework, leaving them feeling exhausted, guilty and unfulfilled. Every week two women were dying as a result of domestic violence.

This was the reality for millions of women even before the worst economic crisis since the 1930s wreaked its havoc around the globe.

What consequences will the crisis and its aftermath have for women? Will the important changes that have already taken place withstand the effects of this dramatic new period or will the film of history begin to unwind? Are inequality, discrimination and oppression an inevitable part of our lives?

This book argues that it doesn't have to be like this. It is true that discrimination and oppression have been in existence for thousands of years. However, as chapter one explains, women have not always been second-class citizens. For the majority of human history we lived in societies where this was not the case. Of course, our conditions of existence are worlds apart today. But if there was a time in the past when oppression did not exist then a future without it is also possible.

But how can we fight back? Should women try and transform themselves, should they try and alter men or is a fundamental change of the economic system needed? Should women fight on their own, together with other women or united with men? Can we change things bit by bit or is a more radical transformation necessary?

We attempt to briefly address all of these questions from a socialist and Marxist point of view and to dispel some of the confusion which surrounds the issue of women's oppression today.

Part One traces the history of women's oppression until the present day. It shows how oppression was connected to the emergence, around 10,000 years ago, of class-based societies in which the family became a basic social structure. It explains how capitalism, the dominant form of class society today, underpins and reinforces the problems which women still continue to face and how ending oppression is linked to ending capitalism and class society.

Part Two looks at how we can organise to fight for women's liberation. It argues that it is important to fight for every improvement possible in the lives of women but, because of the way in which capitalism is structured and organised, real liberation cannot be achieved through gradual reform of the current system. A radical transformation of the way in which society is structured is needed. The main struggle is not one of women against men, or of women changing themselves, but of women organising and uniting with working class men to end capitalism and replace it with a socialist society.

Socialism would transform the lives of women and men. This book gives a glimpse of how life could be different and how another world free from discrimination, inequality and oppression is possible.

part one
a history
of women's
oppression

2 IT DOESN'T HAVE TO BE LIKE THIS

1 Have women always been oppressed?

"Men have broad shoulders and narrow hips, and accordingly they possess intelligence. Women have narrow shoulders and broad hips. Women ought to stay at home; the way they were created indicates this, for they have broad hips and a fundament to sit upon, keep house and bear and raise children."

(Martin Luther, 1531)[1]

For centuries biologically based arguments have been used to portray as 'natural' and 'eternal' inequality and the 'division of labour' between men and women – with women having responsibility for children and the family and men being the economic providers.

Today, most women would burst out laughing if they were told that they earn less money than men because they have broad hips, because their brains are smaller or because of their reproductive organs. Science and social attitudes have moved on! But, even in the 21st century, evolutionary psychologists tell us that 'universal' behaviours such as male promiscuity, rape and violence against women, and even men not ironing, are determined by our genes, which are the product of natural selection. The arguments may have become more 'sophisticated' but the idea that 'biology is destiny' has not disappeared.

In the 1970s, the women's movement set itself the goal of challenging male dominance in all its forms and had an important effect on attitudes and social policy. But some radical feminist ideas were themselves rooted in biological differences between men and women – focusing on women's 'caring' and 'nurturing' natures and men's 'violence' and 'aggression'. Other strands of feminism eschewed these more extreme forms of biological determinism. They concentrated instead on social structures – in particular patriarchy, which has many different definitions but can be summed up as the institutionalised dominance of women by men in society. But whether they focus on biology or social structures or a combination of both, most feminist theories view male supremacy as universal and having existed for all time, regardless of the economic basis of society. Socialists and Marxists, however, argue that the oppression which women experience today has not always existed but is rooted in the rise of societies based on private property and divided into classes – a process which began to take place around 10,000 years ago.

These differences might appear at first sight to be hair-splitting, with little relevance for the struggle today. But that is not the case. For socialists and Marxists, theory is a guide to action – to changing what is wrong with the world. If patriarchy exists as a social structure independent of class society, then the conclusion could be drawn that the main struggle, perhaps even the only struggle, that needs to be waged is one by women against men. This has in fact been the position of many feminists. Socialists and Marxists, however, view male dominance, both in its origin and in its current form, as intrinsically linked to the structures and inequalities of class society. The main struggle is therefore a class struggle, in which the struggles by women against their own specific oppression dovetail with those of the working class in general for a fundamental restructuring of society to end all inequality and oppression.

The origin of the family

The most famous Marxist contribution to the discussion of women's oppression is the *Origin of the Family, Private Property and the State*, which was written by Friedrich Engels, Karl Marx's closest political collaborator. Published in 1884, the ideas in this book were politically explosive – challenging not just the prevailing ideology about the roles of men and women in society but the whole social system itself.

In the *Origin of the Family*, Engels took the Marxist method of historical materialism and applied it to existing archaeological, anthropological and historical evidence to develop his revolutionary ideas on how and why women came to be oppressed and how they could be liberated. He argued that people's social arrangements and the institutions, ideas and values in society are products of particular historical circumstances. So, for example, the family unit of male head of household and economically dependent wife and children was not, as existing capitalist ideology maintained, a natural, eternal and unchanging institution. Societies had existed where the 'bourgeois family', as it was known, had not been the basic unit of society – other social arrangements had predominated and women were not systematically oppressed.

When the economic basis of society changes, wrote Engels – when new methods of production develop – then institutions and beliefs also change, albeit in a complex and non-mechanical way. And if this had been the case in the past then it could also be the case in the future. A transformation in the economic basis of society from capitalism to socialism would in turn alter social relations and lay the basis for ending all social inequalities and achieving the liberation of women.

These were powerful arguments which undermined official ideology – representing capitalist institutions as fixed and unchanging – and potentially threatened the continued existence of the capitalist system itself which relies on unequal social relations, including those between men and women in the family and in society generally, to maintain the status quo.[2]

Engels wrote the *Origin of the Family* over 120 years ago when archaeological and anthropological evidence was extremely scant in comparison with today. Inevitably some of the details which he outlines in the book have been proven incorrect in the light of subsequent scientific advances.[3] Nevertheless, research by anthropologists over the years has vindicated the general thrust of Engels' analysis.[4] There is ample evidence to show that societies existed in the past which were not organised on the basis of private property and the division of society into classes; where there were no institutionalised hierarchical and exploitative social relations and women were not systematically dominated or oppressed by men.

Such societies are usually referred to as 'hunter-gatherer', because of their economic basis, and account for 99% of human history. The basic social organisation of these societies was the kinship group – whose size would vary depending on the environment. While most people in the group would be biologically related to each other, this was not necessarily the case. These were subsistence economies, with members of the group producing just enough to satisfy their immediate needs, and in general they were organised around a division of labour based on sex with men hunting and women gathering fruit, nuts, berries, etc. Women also usually had the main responsibility for childcare.

Division of labour

Despite clear evidence backing up Engels' core argument that class-based societies and women's oppression have only existed for a fraction of humanity and that conditions can change, this has not gone unchallenged. Strands of sociology have argued that since this division of labour existed in early societies, and men and women have continued to assume different roles throughout history, these differences must have a genetic base; that they represent behaviour which is the result of genes which have been selected over time because of their importance for the survival of the species.

So it is natural, therefore, and socially expedient, that men should go out to work and 'hunt' to provide for the family while women stay at home and look after the children and the household. At the same time, 'man the hunter' is by nature aggressive, competitive, dominant and promiscuous while women are genetically programmed to be nurturing, passive and monogamous.

Some feminists have also attributed women's oppression to innate male aggression and the fact that men are physically more powerful than women and therefore able to assert control over them, particularly over their sexuality.[5]

Sociobiologists often refer to aggressive and dominant behaviour in other animals to back up their arguments. However, studies of animals including primates (such as baboons and chimpanzees who share over 90% of our genetic makeup) show that animals display a vast variety of behaviours which are influenced by their environment and subject to change. All of human behaviour is biologically based and biology places certain limits on what we can and cannot do. Human beings, for example, are not born with wings and therefore cannot naturally fly in the way that birds can. Nevertheless, our culture has enabled us to develop the technology to manufacture aeroplanes which allow us to overcome our biological constraints and fly all over the world. It is this cultural evolution, which is the consequence of our ability to labour and control our natural environment, which distinguishes us from other animals and is the most important factor influencing most human behaviour.[6]

The picture that is usually painted of early societies is one of an aggressive male striding off alone with his spear in order to hunt down ferocious wild beasts and then come back to camp, victorious, with food to feed his dependent wife and children who are patiently waiting for him. Evidence of hunter-gatherer societies which have continued into the modern era suggests, in fact, that this is a false picture. Hunting, when it took place, was not generally a solitary, aggressive pursuit but involved group members cooperating together to stalk and catch their prey. There was often flexibility in the tasks which people undertook. In many societies women were in fact involved in scavenging and hunting, particularly if they were not pregnant or nursing small children. And men would also play a role in caring for children. Gathering foodstuffs such as fruit and nuts (which accounted for the majority of the diet of hunter-gatherer societies) often involved women travelling long distances away from the group's base.

In modern capitalist society, the system in which we currently live, the fact that women give birth to, and have the main responsibility for bringing up, children can place them at a big economic and social disadvantage. Lack of adequate or affordable childcare means that working-class women in particular are forced into part-time, low-paid, low-status insecure jobs. Taking time off to have children can seriously harm women's future job prospects. Low pay and insecurity can make it difficult for women to leave unhappy relationships and when they do, they can face severe economic hardship as a lone parent.

Some feminists have drawn the conclusion that women were similarly disadvantaged in early societies because of the division of labour between men and women. But, although in general, women and men carried out different tasks, this does not mean that women were necessarily disadvantaged or that their work and the contribution they made to the group were devalued or considered inferior to those of men. Studies suggest that hunter-gatherer societies were organised on a cooperative, collective basis in which everyone's contribution was valued and respected. Women and children were not economically dependent on a single male provider, all members of the group were dependent on each other for their economic survival, sharing and working together. So if a couple split up (and personal relations were quite fluid) women and children would not necessarily be economically disadvantaged in any way. Looking after children was considered a common responsibility which benefited the whole group and not that of an individual, private family.

Although some individuals might have had more prestige or influence within the group due to their wisdom, experience and ability, decision-making was collective with people making decisions about the activities for which they were responsible.[7] Individuals were not in a position to enforce their will on others, including men over women.

Why did it all go wrong?

In the *Origin of the Family*, Engels argued that the "world historic defeat of the female sex" came about as a result of processes unleashed by revolutionary changes in methods of production – that is the domestication of animals and the cultivation of crops. A radical transformation in production and technique meant that group members no longer had to live from hand to mouth, hunting and gathering foodstuffs, but had the potential to produce over and above their immediate needs. This in turn led to the development of private ownership of the means of producing wealth, the division of society into classes of exploiters and exploited and a state apparatus to maintain the economic control of the ruling class. Women's oppression was intimately bound up with these developments which involved the rise of the nuclear, patriarchal (male-dominated) family.

Although Engels made some mistakes in relation to detail, anthropologists agree that hunter-gatherer societies underwent a radical transformation around 8-10,000 years ago, based on their newly discovered ability to domesticate animals and cultivate crops. This is often referred to as the Neolithic revolution – which like all revolutions was a process and not a single event, in this case taking place over thousands of years and arising independently in several parts of the world. Whereas previously most groups were compelled to move around to secure the foodstuffs they needed to survive, they were now able to stay in one place which led to a big growth in population.

Now that they could produce over and above their day-to-day requirements it was possible for some members of the group to withdraw from production and to specialise in particular tasks. Groups and individuals became responsible for storing, guarding and distributing the surplus, for trade and warfare and for organising production, which conferred on them a certain prestige and status. To begin with, these tasks would have been carried out on behalf of the group as a whole. But it was from amongst these prestigious groups, individuals and households that, in some societies, the first exploiting classes arose as, over time, the wealth at their disposal, and the means of producing it, came to be considered their own private property which they could pass on to their own descendants.

Women's oppression

The general division of labour by sex had not disadvantaged women in the communal kinship group. But as this economic and social transformation unfolded it was those tasks undertaken by men – organising production through irrigation and ploughing, trading, administering the surplus, etc. – which lay the basis for both class rule and the systematic oppression of women (although of course not all men formed part of the ruling class). This was a lengthy, complicated and contradictory process, however, as new social forces and structures came into conflict with the old collective and communal ways of organising society. It was as part of this process that individual households came to replace the kinship group as the main economic and social unit, with women becoming economically dependent and under the control and authority of men within the family. Over time this oppression became systematised and legitimised as a state apparatus developed.

So women's oppression and class society have not developed as separate structures, but are interlinked, rooted in the same economic and social developments that took place thousands of years ago. Capitalism, the current dominant form of class society, has incorporated some of the social structures and ideology which existed in previous class societies, including the family and the second-class status of women. These have formed an essential part of the state apparatus in order to maintain the capitalists' economic and social dominance. However, these have not remained unchanged, either compared to previous feudal or other class societies or as capitalism itself has developed over the past 300 years or so, but have instead been modified and adapted by economic, social and political processes. And, as the family and women's position in society have changed, they have in turn impacted on wider social developments.

2 The role of the family

The word 'family' comes from the Latin word 'familia' – meaning the total number of slaves belonging to one man. It's not just the word, however, that can be traced back to Roman slave society (an early form of class society) but many of the laws which have governed the family in capitalist society in Western Europe and elsewhere. In fact, most of the discrimination and oppression which women continue to experience today cannot be fully understood unless placed in that historical context.

The 'patriarchal' family of the ruling slave-owning class in Roman times was a hierarchical economic and social institution which invested in the male head of household, the 'paterfamilias', total authority over his wife, children, apprentices and slaves – including control over whether they should live or die. Economic production, based on the ownership and exploitation of slaves, was organised through the family, which was also a means of passing on wealth to male descendants of the ruling class. While couples who married might feel some love and affection for each other, marriage for the ruling, slave-owning class was primarily concerned with forming alliances with other families in order to increase their wealth and status.

Marriage and divorce played a similar role for the landowning aristocracy under feudalism, the class society which replaced slavery. Its main purpose was to obtain new land and allies and enhance the power and wealth of the ruling elite. Songs and tales from the Middle Ages frequently referred to love as something quite separate from marriage. Similarly, with industrialisation the rising capitalist class used marriage as a means of consolidating and extending capital and furthering their economic and political ambitions. This didn't mean that couples had no feelings for each other, but marriage was mainly viewed as another business contract. Marriage and the family were important for inheritance, for passing on wealth to legal heirs, and divorce laws were primarily centred on dividing and allocating property. This has continued to be the case in most countries, with even children treated as the 'property' of parents by the courts.

For those who were not from the ruling class, however, family reality was very different. Slaves in Roman society not only had no property, they were property themselves, forbidden by law to marry. Couples could be separated from each other and from their children, and personal relationships ripped apart whenever a slave owner decided to sell his property. In the same way, as capitalism developed, the emerging working class, unlike the capitalist class, had no economic wealth to extend and consolidate or for its children to inherit.

However, in general, the ruling classes throughout history have held up their own family arrangements as the ideal, to be emulated by other classes in society. As the dominant economic class, they have also controlled the legal system, religion, science, education and ideas generally, and used this control to consolidate and perpetuate their economic rule.

Sexual commodities

In Roman times, women were in effect commodities to be exchanged through marriage and divorce. Until they married they were the property of their father and then authority and control passed to their husbands. Husbands expected complete obedience from their wives and this was enshrined in the legal system. Early marriage laws "oblige the married women, as having no other refuge, to conform themselves entirely to the temper of the husbands and the husbands to rule their wives as necessary and inseparable possessions".[1] Whereas men were engaged in the 'public' arena of politics, business, culture, etc., women's role in society was normally confined to the family and the 'private' sphere with restrictions placed on their appearance in public places. Women of the ruling class had the responsibility of overseeing and managing the household where their main function was to give birth to and raise the children who would inherit property and wealth. This was very different from hunter-gatherer societies where women's caring role was a public not a private function but carried out for the benefit of the whole kinship group and not an individual family.

Whereas women in early pre-class societies experienced sexual freedom and relationships were quite flexible, in slave society women's sexuality was heavily regulated and controlled, backed up by religion and the law. The worst crime that a woman of the ruling class could commit was adultery (adultery by women of other classes was not considered a problem). This was because men wanted to be able to guarantee the paternity of the children who would inherit their property – something completely unnecessary in egalitarian communal society where there was no private ownership of the means of producing wealth. In Roman times, adultery, defined as sexual activity between a married woman and a man not her husband, was a crime against property (as was rape) punishable by divorce and even death.

The Roman censor Cato summed up this double standard in one of his speeches: "If you should take your wife in adultery, you may with impunity put her to death without a trial – but if you should commit adultery or indecency, she must not presume to lay a finger on you, nor does the law allow it."[2] Severe punishments were also meted out to women who drank wine, walked unveiled in the street, made poisons and any other behaviour which could lead to their committing adultery or aborting an unborn child. Men, on the other hand, were not expected to be monogamous and regularly took concubines or went with prostitutes. Prostitution in fact developed as the 'other side' of the monogamous (for women) family.

Controlling women

All over the world, since the existence of class society, various controls and restraints have been placed on women's bodies and sexual freedom – from the wearing of the veil, to foot binding and the brutal practice of female genital mutilation aimed at denying women sexual pleasure.

Today, many of the most severe restrictions to which women are subjected internationally have become associated with Islam. In fact, Islam, which arose in the seventh century in Arabia, was quite enlightened in relation to women's rights given the prevailing attitudes to women at that time in most of the world. According to the Koran, women were permitted to inherit property, were expected to enjoy sex and had the right to divorce if they did not – rights which women in Europe were still fighting for well into the 19th century.

Practices such as the wearing of the veil, honour killings or female genital mutilation are not specific to Islam but have also been imposed by other religions such as Hinduism and Christianity. Women's sexuality was being controlled long before the rise of Islam, from the time that the first class societies emerged. But as Islam spread throughout the world, it adopted practices which were already being enforced in the conquered territories, and then integrated and incorporated them in the interests of the ruling elite. In all class societies religion has been used by the economically-dominant class to legitimise inequality and oppression in order to maintain its economic and social control.

The Koran is the product of the society and times in which it was written and it is open to many different interpretations. The right-wing fundamentalist rule of the Taliban in Afghanistan, for example, enforced a brutal oppression of women. There, and in other countries, women have risked their lives to fight against restrictions imposed by reactionary theocratic regimes, including the wearing of the burqa.

The veil is historically a symbol of oppression which progressive women, including in Muslim societies, have fought against. However, it is not necessarily viewed as oppressive by all Muslim women who wear it in the West. There are many reasons why they might freely choose to wear the hijab (or, more rarely, the full veil or niqab); as a means of asserting their identity in the face of increased racism and Islamophobia; as a statement of solidarity with Muslims facing oppression around the world or as an act of defiance against imperialist aggression. Some also view it as empowering and liberating – a reaction against a capitalist society which objectifies women – forcing people to see them as individuals and not as merely bodies or sex objects.

Socialists and Marxists oppose and expose the role that all organised religions have historically played, and continue to play today, in maintaining inequality, exploitation and oppression. At the same time, we support an individual's right to freedom of religious expression. Women should not be forced to wear the veil against their will but they should also have the right to wear it if they choose to. So we have supported the struggles by women in Iran, for example, for democratic, religious and personal freedoms and those of young female Muslims in France and other parts of Europe for the right to be able to wear the headscarf in schools and workplaces. We have also backed the struggles of women in western countries who have challenged the role of the Catholic Church in denying women reproductive rights.

Violence against women

Under capitalism the stereotypical representations of women which abound in the media, advertising and general culture have their roots in the rise of class society.[3] The same is true of violence against women. Worldwide, women aged 15-44 are more likely to be maimed or die from violence at the hands of men than from cancer, malaria, traffic accidents or war combined. Even in the developed industrialised countries a quarter of women at some time in their lives will suffer from domestic violence.

Many reasons have been advanced in an effort to explain why this abuse still continues today at such a high level.

Some people blame economic problems such as unemployment and bad working conditions. But such a crude 'economic reductionist' explanation is completely inadequate. Domestic violence takes place across all social classes and is not just confined to the poor and the working class. Alcohol is also often cited as a cause. However, while some perpetrators are abusive after drinking alcohol others are violent while completely sober. Alcohol, like unemployment, long working hours and the general pressures and strains of life in capitalist society can contribute to and trigger domestic abuse but they are not the underlying cause.

Women also suffer from stress. In fact, it could be argued that, as working-class women usually have to juggle work and assume most of the responsibility of looking after children and the home, their lives are even more stressful than those of men. Sometimes women will themselves resort to violence within relationships but the overwhelming majority of domestic violence is perpetrated by men against women.

So why is it that men feel justified in using violence in situations where women normally do not? Male abusers often seek to justify their behaviour by blaming the women themselves; they provoked them by "nagging", by not getting a meal on the table in time, not keeping the house clean, or the children quiet. As a consequence, many women who experience domestic violence, especially if the abuse continues over a period of years, come to believe incorrectly that the violence is their own fault. They may then try to modify their behaviour, to avoid anything which might 'provoke' the abuser, but the violence and abuse does not stop; in fact in many cases it escalates.

From the 'excuses' given by male perpetrators it is clear that traditional beliefs about the need for women to be loyal and obedient to their husbands, and men having the right to use fear and coercion to keep them 'in their place', still influence behaviour and attitudes today. The hierarchical, patriarchal family based on male authority and control served the economic and social needs of the ruling slave-owning class in Roman times. And the family has continued as a social institution central to all class societies, although its form, of course, has not remained the same.

In the feudal societies of mediæval Europe, for example, the family of the landowning aristocracy was organised differently to that of the peasant/serf household which was an economic unit at the centre of production of goods consumed by themselves and the Lord of the Manor. Feudal society was hierarchical with God at the top and the peasants/serfs at the bottom of the pile. Everyone knew their place in a rigid order based on obedience to authority and unequal rights and responsibilities. The patriarchal peasant family, with male authority sanctioned by the legal system and legitimised by God and King, both reflected and reinforced the hierarchy of society in general and functioned as a means of social control. The double oppression peasant women suffered was clearly reflected in the Lord's right to bed a bride on her wedding night.

For centuries men have been legally and morally obliged to control the behaviour of their wives. It was perfectly legitimate, in fact expected, that a husband would use physical coercion against a 'nagging' wife or one who failed to fulfil her 'wifely obligations'. Laws that did exist were mainly concerned with setting limits on how far they could go. For example, the English saying "rule of thumb" is thought to stem from the fact that it used to be stipulated that the thickness of the stick used by a man to beat his wife could not be greater than his thumb.

In Britain in 1736, a dictum from Sir Matthew Hale, the head of the judiciary, stated that rape in marriage could not take place because "by their mutual matrimonial consent and contract the wife hath given herself in this kind to her husband which she cannot retract".

Such ideas became deeply embedded in society over centuries. It was only in the early 1990s in Britain that the Law Commission declared marital rape illegal. Prior to that, the idea that women's bodies became the property of men on marriage still prevailed in law. Although there has been a big shift in social attitudes in relation to domestic violence and rape over the last few decades, backward ideas still hold sway. There is still reluctance, for example, on the part of the criminal justice system to prosecute in cases of marital rape, and the courts often view it as less serious than rape by a stranger.

Capitalism itself is a hierarchical system, based on inequality and exploitation by a minority in society. The ruling capitalist class will resort to violence if necessary to maintain its rule – by the use of the police against striking workers and protesters, for example, or the armed forces in wars for profit and prestige. The capitalist system of inequality, dominance and control, in which the family plays a crucial role, permeates the whole of society including personal relations, resting on and perpetuating backward ideas which originated in the early class societies thousands of years ago.[4]

3 The family under capitalism

One of the most significant changes to the family as an institution, which in turn had an important effect on the position of women in society generally, came about as a consequence of industrialisation and the rise of capitalism.

In pre-industrial society, individual families that did not form part of the ruling economic class were mostly centres of economic production, organised through the male head of household. Whether domestic production was geared towards manufacture or agriculture, the work of women, although extremely arduous, was central. Although the division of labour between men and women was clearly unequal, no distinction was made between the value of tasks which women performed, such as spinning, childcare, cleaning or agricultural work – all were carried out in and around the home and all were considered productive and necessary work. But with industrialisation, goods previously produced in the home such as food, drink and clothing were now socially produced in the factories and mills – although ownership of the means of production was in private hands.

This had a big effect on the family and on personal relations. In the early stages of factory production women and children were the main labourers sought by the capitalists. This created a clear division between the paid work that women carried out in the workplace, where they were brutally exploited in barbaric conditions, and the unpaid work of cleaning, cooking, caring for children, etc., which women continued to perform in the home as they had traditionally done.

In an economic system in which wage labour predominated, this unwaged domestic work was devalued and in turn impacted on women in the workplace, where they were devalued as workers, paid lower wages than men and suffered inferior working conditions. Even when working-class women toiled in the workplace, their main function in society was still considered to be that of wife, mother and homemaker.

Wage labour

Once women became wage labourers in the factories they secured a degree of economic independence which to a certain extent undermined male authority within the family. In fact, with economic production organised in the factory under the control of the capitalists, it appeared that the material basis for patriarchal control in the working-class family no longer existed.

As Engels explained: "Here there is no property, for the preservation and inheritance of which monogamy and male supremacy were established; hence there is no incentive to make male supremacy prevail... and now that large-scale industry has taken the wife out of the home onto the labour market and into the factory, and made her often the breadwinner of the family, the last remnants of male supremacy in the proletarian household are deprived of all foundation, except, perhaps, for a leftover piece of the brutality towards women that has become deep-rooted since the introduction of monogamy."[1]

Nevertheless, despite the enormous economic and social upheavals that industrialisation unleashed, the patriarchal family not only survived but became strengthened as the newly-emerged capitalist class attempted to use its economic, legal and ideological control to mould it in the interests of its own class rule.

In the course of the 19th century it became increasingly a sign of the growing wealth of the capitalist class that their wives did not work outside the home but were economically dependent on a male breadwinner. One of the bourgeois woman's main roles was to tend to the emotional needs of her husband – the so-called 'angel in the house' – leaving men free to engage in industry, finance, politics, etc. in the public sphere. Women's other role centred around reproduction – bearing and rearing the future ruling class. It was a sign of respectability for the capitalist class, marking it off from the 'dissolute' aristocracy and the 'feckless' working class.

The situation was very different for the working class itself. When industrialisation first began it was far from clear that capitalism – unstable and crisis ridden – would last as an economic system. Women and very young children were in many cases literally worked to death in the 'dark, satanic mills' as the capitalists squeezed every last drop of profit from their labour. Brutalised, toiling for unbearably long hours in dangerous conditions in exchange for wages barely enough to stave off starvation, they returned exhausted to disease infested, overcrowded slums.

It was impossible for women to care adequately for children in such terrible conditions. Babies and small children were often left with other siblings and given gin and opium to silence their cries. Levels of infant mortality were extremely high and family life virtually non-existent. "It is quite common for women to be working in the evening and for the child to be delivered the following morning and it is no means uncommon for babies to be born in the factory itself among the machinery," wrote Engels in the *Condition of the Working Class in England*. "It is often only two or three days after confinement that a woman returns to the factory, and of course, she cannot take the baby with her."

Concerned only with short-term profits, individual capitalists brutally resisted working-class struggles to improve their working and daily lives. But as capitalism stabilised, the more farsighted sections of the capitalist class took a longer-term view. Realising that the system as a whole would benefit from having a healthier and more educated workforce, they were prepared to grant some concessions to the working class. Amongst the earliest reforms were protective laws enacted in the 1830s which restricted the hours and labour of women and children in the factories. At the same time, it became clear that the family, which seemed to be disintegrating amongst the working class, had an important role to play in maintaining existing workers and nurturing the next generation of workers to produce profits for the capitalist class.

Economic and ideological role

The capitalist system could reap the benefits of a healthier and more educated working-class but the capitalists wanted to achieve this with as little cost to themselves as possible. It suited their interests for individual working-class families to take on this responsibility, and to feed, clothe and care for all 'unproductive' members – all those whose labour power could not be exploited in the workplace – such as young children, the elderly, the sick, the disabled, the unemployed – - with no recourse to the state.

The capitalists also required a workforce that was disciplined, obedient and deferential to authority. The patriarchal family, in which men had control over women and children, including through the use of physical violence, was a useful institution for instilling these values and for promoting appropriate gender roles. The family was also a means of disciplining working-class men themselves. It was an enormous burden for men to assume responsibility for providing economically for all dependent family members. The capitalists exploited this responsibility during strikes, for example, in an attempt to force strikers back to work.

Through their control of the legal system, religion, education and ideas in general the ruling classes of the main capitalist countries promoted the bourgeois family – with women responsible for the home and nurturing children, and economically dependent on the male head of household – as natural, eternal and the model to which all classes in society should aspire. 'Family values' propaganda and periodic 'moral panics' focused on the supposed crisis in working-class families.

Nowhere was this clearer than in Britain, the world's dominant capitalist power by the end of the 19th Century. The ruling class required healthy and fit working-class men to serve as cannon fodder for the British Empire. The poor health of potential recruits and poverty in general was blamed on 'inadequate' and 'feckless' working-class mothers who failed in their nurturing and mothering duties – a convenient scapegoat for an unequal economic system that was incapable of meeting the most basic needs of working-class people.

The physical and moral health of the nation and the British Empire were equated with the health of the family. But the only family considered morally healthy was the heterosexual bourgeois family, and the state encouraged intolerance and repression of anything that seem to challenge or undermine it. Women who gave birth to illegitimate children, for example, were punished with the workhouse. In 1885 homosexuality was criminalised for the first time and in 1895 the playwright Oscar Wilde was sentenced to two years hard labour for 'gross indecency'.

There was no corresponding legislation against lesbianism. It was not considered to exist as women were not thought to have sexual desires and urges. Sexuality in general was meant to be repressed in the interests of reproduction, wealth creation and capital accumulation. The infamous Contagious Diseases Acts viciously repressed women who were deemed responsible for the spread of venereal disease. Any working-class woman could be identified as a "common prostitute" and forced to undergo internal examinations and locked up in hospital if found to be suffering from gonorrhoea or syphilis.

The 'ideal' family

By the end of the 19th century, the ruling class had become relatively successful in ideologically establishing the bourgeois family as the ideal family form. Part of this success was due to the fact that the bourgeois family model appeared to coincide with the material interests of working-class people themselves. They wanted to change the desperate conditions which they were forced to work and live in. The reasoning went that if married women did not have to work long hours outside the home it would be better for them, and they would have more time for domestic tasks and for caring for children and other family members – consequently improving all of their lives.

The idea of a 'family wage', which would be paid to a male head of household and would be sufficient to meet the needs of the whole family, gained support amongst the working class. But in reality only a section of skilled working-class men managed to achieve it. In many households, wages were so low that all family members were compelled to work in order to survive. Women who were widowed, deserted or on their own for whatever reason had no choice but to work, although a single female wage was often barely enough to prevent starvation.

Married women continued to work outside the home, did piecework at home or took in lodgers or other people's laundry. But at the same time, they were expected to clean, prepare meals and cater for all the physical and emotional needs of other family members, without of course the maids and servants which ruling-class and many middle-class families had. This 'double burden', together with numerous pregnancies and births, took an enormous toll on working-class women's health and lives.

So in fact, for the working class family reality fell way short of the supposed ideal. Nevertheless, ideologically the bourgeois family has permeated the whole of capitalist society, shaping legislation and attitudes. Its durability is due to the dual role which the family plays. On the one hand, it is an economic and social institution which fulfils a vital economic and ideological function for the capitalist class. But at the same time it is a site of personal relations that are central to most people's lives. Although the family is often a place of inequality, violence and abuse, it also meets people's needs for love, companionship and emotional support, as well as economic support. But under capitalism these two roles constantly come into conflict, causing tensions and contradictions that capitalism is incapable of resolving.

Welfare responsibility

Poverty wages and insecure employment meant that it was impossible for individual working-class families to meet even the most basic needs of all of their members. They lived in desperate fear of being struck down by unemployment, sickness or disability. Children were malnourished and child mortality rates extremely high. Women suffered countless pregnancies which ruined their health and they often died in childbirth. Prostitution flourished and old age could mean total destitution. In England at the end of the 19th century social investigators like Charles Booth lifted the lid on the terrible poverty of the working-class. His report on the East End of London found that 35% were 'poor' and a third of those were suffering from acute 'distress'. When mobilisation took place for the Boer War the ruling class became acutely aware of the how the physical condition of working-class men had been undermined by years of poverty and neglect. As many as 40% of men called up were deemed physically unfit to fight.[2]

In an attempt to survive and to provide some kind of protection against the disasters and problems of everyday life, sections of the working class united together in organisations such as trade unions, friendly societies and cooperatives. But at the same time they fought for the state to assume collective responsibility for education, health and the welfare of all those who were unable to provide for themselves, rather than the responsibility falling on individual families who did not have the resources to cope.

It was against the backdrop of growing class struggles and/or the fear of revolution that the ruling class in some countries moved to introduce the beginnings of a welfare state. So in Britain, for example, the Liberal government of Lloyd George initiated national insurance and other reforms in 1911 at a time of heightened class struggle. The National Health Service itself, which was implemented by a Labour government in 1948, came about because the ruling class faced an angry and militant post-war working class which was not prepared to return to the miseries of the past and was demanding a better future.

Although often far short of what was needed to provide a decent standard of living, state pensions, sickness and unemployment benefit, child and maternity benefits all relieved some of the insecurities and financial burdens placed on individual working-class families. The provision of public housing, health care, nurseries, facilities for elderly people and the disabled made an enormous difference to the lives of working-class people, especially women.

However, although the state began to carry out some of the tasks that had previously been carried out by the family, the idea of the traditional nuclear family, with a male breadwinner and economically dependent wife, continued to underpin most welfare policy. In Britain, for example, women did not have an individual right to some state benefits, the assumption being that they would be provided for by their husbands, thus reinforcing the patriarchal family. The welfare state also differentiated between 'deserving' and 'undeserving' poor, with widows receiving higher benefits than divorcees, for example.

Nevertheless, the existence of the welfare state transformed the lives of many women. It lifted some of their domestic burden, allowing them to work outside the home. In fact, the welfare state itself became a major employer of female labour, with women making up the overwhelming majority of teachers, nurses, carers, etc. In those countries where public housing and minimal benefits have existed, women have been able to leave unhappy relationships and have some form of economic independence, however inadequate.

At the same time, as a consequence of struggles by women and the working class in general, and changing public attitudes, women in many countries have gained easier access to divorce, as well as free contraception and abortion rights. Having some control over when and whether to have children has given women more freedom of choice, allowing them more independence and greater access to education and to work outside the home.

Women in the workplace

In the *Origin of the Family*, Engels wrote that the first condition for the liberation of women is to bring the "whole female sex" back into public industry. Paid work outside the home weakens the economic and financial dependency of women on individual men within the family and gives them the confidence to challenge traditional ideas about their role in society. When women are isolated in the home caring for children, consumed by the monotony of housework, it is easy to feel that all the problems of daily life are personal and individual and to blame themselves for everything that is happening to them. Breaking down that isolation, working alongside others in the workplace broadens women's horizons and it becomes easier to view these as social rather than individual problems. Although the capitalist class do everything in their power to sow divisions amongst working-class people along the lines of sex, race, sexuality, etc., it is in the workplace that the potential for collective struggle for change is clearest.

Since the industrial revolution working-class women have always worked outside the home. But that work was considered secondary to their main domestic role within the family. This enabled the capitalist class to justify paying women lower wages in order to exploit them as cheap labour to boost their profits. But capitalist ideology has varied, depending on the ruling classes' economic and social needs at any particular time. So in the First and Second World Wars, for example, the capitalist class needed women to labour in the munitions factories and to do the jobs left vacant by the men who had been mobilised to fight at the front. They encouraged and sometimes compelled women, including married women with children, to go into the labour market and to take on work from which they had been previously excluded; and these women proved in practice that they were just as capable as male workers. State propaganda informed women that it was their 'patriotic duty' to work outside the home. "Men trenches; women benches", declared one slogan in Britain during the First World War. (3) During that war, nearly one and a half million women flooded into the workplaces and over two million during the Second World War, many of them married women with children.

Inevitably, in most cases women were paid a lower rate for the job than men. Male workers, especially in the engineering industry, organised against what became known as 'dilution' – women workers undermining the skills and pay of men. But there were also joint struggles for equal pay as female union membership increased by over 150%. The demand for female labour forced the state to step in and alleviate some of the domestic tasks of women with children. Government grants helped pay for the setting up of local authority day nurseries and there were big improvements in maternity care. But when war was over the propaganda changed again. With millions of men returning home after 1918, it was now women's 'patriotic duty' to give up their jobs to unemployed men. A stable family life was deemed necessary to increase the birth rate and rebuild the country after the devastation of war. The day nurseries closed down and tens of thousands of women found themselves back in the isolation of the home and economically dependent on their husbands.

Over a million women also lost their jobs when the Second World War came to a close, although it was now considered acceptable for married women to work part-time. This suited the need of the capitalist class for cheap labour in the post-war economic upswing and a 'reserve army' of labour which could be dispensed with when necessary in periods of economic crisis. And although married women's wages were disparagingly referred to as 'pin money' (and therefore the capitalists felt justified in continuing to pay women a lower rate than men) these wages became essential in maintaining and improving the living standards of working-class families during the boom.

4 The family and women's oppression today

Today women work in unprecedented numbers outside of the home. In fact, in some of the developed capitalist countries they make up half or even a majority of the workforce. And this 'feminisation' of the labour market has been an international phenomenon affecting the neo-colonial countries as well.

In some of the developed countries, the rise of women in the workforce coincided with a decline in male employment – provoking some commentators to suggest that a 'genderquake' had taken place, and that equality was within women's grasp.[1] Others bemoaned a shift in gender relations that was 'going too far', undermining men's traditional role as economic providers and leading to conflict between the sexes.

Claims that women have taken 'men's jobs' are, however, unfounded. A restructuring of capitalism has taken place resulting in a decline in manufacturing industry in many developed countries – a sector historically employing mainly male workers – and a substantial increase in employment in the service sector, in what have traditionally been considered 'women's jobs'.

Of course, in the pursuit of cheap labour, some of that manufacturing industry has been relocated to Eastern Europe and neo-colonial countries where women workers have often been involved in the manufacturing process, particularly in light industry. Multinational companies have been given financial incentives to set up in 'special economic zones' where they can flout basic health and safety and environmental regulations and super-exploit their workforce, with young women considered particularly docile and malleable.

The drawing of women into these industries has certainly had a positive effect on their consciousness and attitudes, just as it has in countries such as Europe and the United States. But the terrible working conditions that they are forced to endure, reminiscent of those of the industrial revolution in the 19th century, show clearly that working outside the home, in and of itself, in no way constitutes liberation.

In the 'advanced' capitalist countries it is undoubtedly the case that a section of better educated, and often middle-class women, have succeeded in securing relatively highly-paid jobs and have made inroads into some professions previously dominated by men such as medicine and law. But deeply ingrained discrimination means that even these women hit their heads against the 'glass ceiling', with the top jobs and pay still going overwhelmingly to men.

For most working-class women, however, they would just like to get off the 'sticky floor'. Not only has the gap between rich and poor widened in most countries over the last few years but there has also been a polarisation amongst women themselves. Working-class women continue to be overwhelmingly segregated in what have become known as the 3 'Cs' – cleaning, catering and caring. Most of these jobs are an extension of the work which they perform unpaid in the home, and as a consequence are low status and low paid. This is one of the main reasons why in many countries, decades after women fought for and won equal pay legislation, their average wages still fall well short of those of male workers. It also leads to a lifetime of poverty and inequality, especially in old age.

Neo-liberal offensive

At the end of the 1970s, in a response to the end of the 1950-73/75 post-war boom and a general economic crisis, including falling profits, the capitalist class began to unleash a neo-liberal offensive which involved vicious attacks on the wages and conditions of the working class. The capitalists have particularly exploited women's caring role in the family as part of their neo-liberal agenda. 'Flexible' working has been promoted as 'family friendly' allowing women to combine paid work with looking after children and the home.

Most working-class women (and men) would welcome flexible working if it meant that they could earn a decent wage, have a secure life and spend quality time with their children. But part-time working and poverty wages mostly go hand in hand. Short-term contracts, temporary work, agency labour, zero hour working are all 'boss friendly' – resulting in super-exploitation and insecurity which places enormous strains on working-class people, affecting personal relationships and family life. And these are often the first jobs to go in an economic recession, sometimes without even the limited safety net of social benefits for those becoming unemployed.

The capitalist class, through their political representatives, have also waged war on the idea of collectively-provided public services, pursuing a brutal agenda of privatisation and cuts. A decent public health service, education system and welfare system are considered vital elements of a decent life by most working-class and middle-class people. As a result of the 'post-war settlement', when governments responded to the demands of a strengthened working class by introducing reforms, public services were paid for by taxing both workers and capitalists. In a situation of high economic growth and increasing profits the capitalists were prepared to go along with this situation in order to buy social peace.

But as profitability declined they demanded cuts in public spending in order that their tax burden could be reduced. At the same time, privatisation opened up new markets for profit-hungry companies to exploit, while, they hoped, weakening the power and organising strength of the trade unions.

Where publicly funded services are cut workers either have to pay for those services privately – which in most cases they cannot afford to do as the capitalists resist raising wages or in some cases cut existing wages – or they are forced to make do as best they can without. Once again working-class families are forced to fall back on their own inadequate resources in order to care for the young, the sick, the elderly and disabled as publicly financed and provided services are run down and slashed.

This can be seen most graphically in a country like Italy where, despite huge and almost revolutionary struggles by the working class in the 1970s, which led to important gains in the workplace and more broadly in society, welfare provision, particularly unemployment benefits, remains extremely inadequate. Young people in low-paid and 'precarious' jobs or without work are forced to remain dependent on their families, with young men in particular often staying at home until well into their thirties. Without the 'cushion' of the family in Italy tens of thousands of young people would be literally destitute.

It is women in particular who bear the brunt of public-sector cuts and privatisation. The high level of women working in the public sector means that it is often their jobs and conditions that are under threat, while cuts in public services add to their burden in the home. If nurseries close down, women are expected to somehow juggle childcare and work. They are expected to look after elderly relatives if affordable residential care is no longer available or to care for disabled family members when state-funded facilities cease to exist.

Divide and rule

Of course, in many households men now shoulder some of the burden. In most countries there have been positive changes in men's attitudes towards the traditional division of labour between men and women. The average amount of housework that men carry out has increased and they are more likely to be involved in looking after their children than in the past. However, opinion polls show a sharp divergence between what men think they should be doing and what they actually do in practice. While men might help out a bit more around the home the vast bulk of housework and childcare is still carried out by women. Even when men and women both work full-time, women still spend more hours looking after children, cleaning, shopping, cooking and carrying out other household chores.

Some feminists have argued that individual men have been the main beneficiaries of this division of labour between the sexes. Clearly, some men have derived some gains such as more leisure time, for example. But being able to spend a few more hours in the gym or the pub pales into insignificance compared to the enormous economic benefits for the capitalist class.

Because services such as childcare, preparing a meal, cleaning, etc. can be bought in the 'market', there have been several attempts to calculate how much the unpaid labour carried out by women in the family actually saves capitalism every year. The figures run into billions – larger even than the entire gross domestic products of the countries surveyed.

The problems that working-class men face under capitalism in general far outweigh any advantages that they might gain in the home. In fact, while the neo-liberal offensive has meant an increase in part-time working for some workers, mainly women, there have also been attacks on the shorter working weeks that other sections of workers have won in the past. Many male workers work intolerably long hours in the workplace, leaving them little time to spend with their families. At the same time other male workers are seeing their jobs 'feminised'.

Throughout history working-class women have struggled to achieve equality in the workplace. The capitalists say they are also in favour of 'equality' between men and women workers. However, their idea of equality is not to bring women's wages and conditions up to those of men but to 'equalise down', pushing working-class men into low-paid, part-time, flexible working in order to boost their profits. In the same way, they use migrant workers, agency workers, subcontractors, etc. to try and force down the wages and conditions of all workers.

In the public sector, male workers are sometimes encouraged to accept cuts in wages and worse conditions in return for promised improvements for low-paid women workers. These divide and rule tactics and attempts at 'sharing out the misery' should be vigorously opposed through a united struggle in the workplace.

In the 1970s, when there were far fewer women in the workforce than today, some women fought for the unpaid tasks of women in the home to be recognised as 'work' and raised the demand of 'wages for housework'. It's certainly important that the value of housework and childcare to capitalism is recognised but 'wages for housework' is in reality a retrograde demand, reinforcing the private nature of household tasks and, at the same time, strengthening backward and stereotypical ideas about women's role in the family and in society generally.

Socialists and Marxists campaign instead for a decent minimum income for carers as well as for pensioners, students and all those unable to work. At the same time, we support the 'socialisation' of many of the tasks currently carried out by individual women in the home. While Engels considered bringing women into "public industry" the first condition for their liberation he crucially added that "this in turn demands the abolition of the monogamous family's attribute of being the economic unit of society". "Private housekeeping," he wrote, "is transformed into a social industry."[2]

'Domestic and personal services' have, in fact, become one of the fastest-growing sectors of the economy in recent years. If the better off can pay for cleaners, gardeners and eat out in fancy restaurants, why should these services not be publicly funded and collectively provided for the benefit of everyone in society, just as health, education and other services have been?[3] However, that would require a fundamental change in the way that society is organised. Because of the structural economic crisis of capitalism the ruling class will continue to attack the economic and social gains that working-class people have won through past struggles. And they will continue to rely on the unpaid labour of women in the family.

Capitalist contradictions

It is one of the contradictions of capitalism that it developed historically as a system that relied on the institution of the family, and therefore sought to strengthen it, but at the same time processes within the capitalist system are simultaneously undermining it. Of course, for all their talk of the importance and sanctity of the family, the ruling class throughout the history of capitalism have readily resorted to policies which damage families if it is deemed to be in capitalism's wider interests. So, for example, in Britain the vicious Poor Law of the early 19th century, which was designed to facilitate a flow of cheap labour into the factories in the cities, ripped apart destitute families as they were thrown into the dreaded Poor House. Today's immigration laws cause terrible pain and suffering for many families. Harsher sentencing by the courts also means that more women are imprisoned for 'economic' crimes such as theft, and separated from their children.

However, for the most part, the changes which have undermined the family as an institution have come about as a consequence of other economic and social changes rather than because of conscious policies. The capitalists' demand for cheap labour and the huge influx of women into the workforce, including women with young children, means that the 'traditional' family of stay-at-home mother and sole male breadwinner now comprises a minority of households in most developed countries. Although processes vary from country to country, in general, divorce and lone parenthood have increased, more couples than ever before are living together rather than getting married and 'reconstituted' families (where people set up new households after divorce or splitting up) are becoming more common.

There are many reasons why relationships break down. Often it is simply because people change or drift apart and need to move on. But there's no doubt that the economic and psychological pressures which capitalism places on the family are an important factor. Long hours and stressful working conditions, money worries, poor housing, the strains of juggling work and family responsibilities all take their toll on personal relationships. Women's economic independence and changing attitudes have also had an effect. In many countries a majority of divorces are initiated by women, a sign that their expectations have changed and that they are less prepared to stay in relationships where they feel unhappy or unfulfilled.

Right reaction

There have been divisions and tensions within the ruling class over how to respond to these changes in the family – often resulting in contradictory policies. In the 1980s, the ideas of the New Right, inspired by the writings of sociologists like Charles Murray, came to prominence in the US and Britain in particular. 'New Right' is a catch-all term incorporating different strands of opinion and groups including free-marketeers and the Christian Right. However, in general they consider that social problems such as crime, truancy and drug abuse are caused by moral decline which is intimately bound up with the decline and disintegration of the patriarchal family.

This is very similar to the 'family values' propaganda of the late 19th century. So, for the New Right, increases in divorce, lone parenthood, 'illegitimacy', etc. are viewed as a crisis which can only be solved by recreating the heterosexual, patriarchal family where women stay at home and perform the role to which they are biologically suited – bearing and raising children – and men are the economic providers and discipliners of dependent wives and children. The New Right advocates policies which strengthen the traditional nuclear family and undermine alternative social arrangements. So, they argue, divorce should be made more difficult so that couples stay together, the tax and benefit system should actively promote marriage while undermining lone parenthood, abortion should be restricted so that women have less control over their sexuality and homosexuality should be totally discouraged.

The ideas of the New Right have had a certain influence over government policy in Britain and the US. Some capitalist political representatives clearly believe that it is possible to legislate and use social policy to alter people's personal behaviour and 'glue the family back together again'. However, most understand that because of changing social attitudes any attempt to 'turn back the clock' would face enormous resistance and would be almost impossible to achieve. Nevertheless, from an ideological point of view family-values propaganda has played an important role. When governments blame working-class parents for truancy and crime committed by young people, for example, this can gain a certain echo. Most parents feel responsible for their families and want to do the best for their children. In a situation where no mainstream parties are putting forward a collective solution to social problems or pointing the finger of blame where it really lies – with a system which places profit first and offers no future to working-class youth – parents can blame themselves and other families when things go wrong.

By scapegoating families in this way the ruling class is able to divert attention away from the crisis of their own system while at the same time sowing divisions and undermining collective struggle for change. In this sense the capitalist class continues to rely on the family as a means of social control.

While they also rely on the family from an economic point of view, governments have not in general actively embarked on a concerted campaign to force women out of the workforce and into the home. On the contrary, the capitalist class's demands for flexible, cheap labour and cuts in welfare have often resulted in policies aimed at getting more and more economically inactive women into the workforce. In a situation of economic crisis and recession, of course, many women will lose those jobs, especially where the service sector is hit particularly hard. But because women's work is central to the capitalist economy, and because women now see themselves as a permanent part of the workforce, when job losses occur they are normally as a result of a generalised attack on jobs and services rather than one specifically targeted at women workers themselves.

Because getting lone parents off of benefits and into work fits in with the need to cut back on public spending, governments in Britain and the US in particular have aimed policies at lone parents who have been less likely to be in work. Many lone parents would welcome the opportunity to be able to work outside the home but only if they are earning sufficient wages to allow them and their children to have a decent standard of living, and if they know that their children are being well looked after. However, most lone parents have been pushed into low-paid, insecure jobs, working for wages not that much higher than benefit level. Childcare, where it exists, is overwhelmingly concentrated in the private sector where the drive for profit takes precedence over quality care. Those lone parents who are unable to work because of health or other problems (or because jobs simply don't exist where they live) are left to survive as best they can on totally inadequate or in some cases non-existent benefits.

While there have been some 'carrots' in the form of tax credits to top up low wages and help with childcare, governments have also wielded a 'big stick', threatening, and in some cases going ahead with, cuts in benefits in order to force lone parents to take up work. 'Family values' propaganda – holding up marriage and two-parent families as the best and most stable way of bringing up children – has played an important role in 'softening up' public opinion prior to cuts in benefits and public services.

However, this has not been a straightforward process. When the New Labour government first came to power in Britain in 1997 and launched an attack on lone-parent benefits they were forced to retreat in the face of a wave of fierce opposition.

Changing social attitudes

The shift in social attitudes that has occurred in many countries means that there is generally now a more tolerant attitude towards alternative social arrangements which do not correspond to the 'traditional' family form. To a certain extent capitalist ideology has adapted to incorporate these changes. Realising that there are few votes to be gained in overtly bashing lone parents, and that it can be counterproductive, all of the mainstream parties in Britain softened their tone, insisting that they did not want to stigmatise lone parents, who, they patronisingly declare, do an excellent job in difficult conditions. Attacks are instead repackaged as 'helping lone parents to help themselves'.

Several governments have legalised same-sex marriages and civil partnerships and granted more rights to same-sex couples with regards to adoption. If capitalism were about to experience an unprecedented economic upswing, much greater even than that after the Second World War, then theoretically it might be possible to organise society in such a way that it no longer needed the family as an economic and ideological prop. It would then be possible to accommodate social changes affecting the family and personal relations without these being seen as a crisis which needs to be 'solved'.

But that is clearly not the perspective facing capitalism – on the contrary the system is in a severe crisis with the general curve of capitalist development going downwards. Of course, within that general downswing there will be periodic economic upturns, some of which can even last several years. But the underlying crisis of profitability means growth is likely to be weak and fragile. This, together with the enormous 'debt overhang' of both consumers and governments, means that the capitalist class will intensify their vicious attacks on the 'social wage' – the very benefits and public services which working-class people have fought so hard for in order to ease some of the stresses and insecurities which dominate their lives, and which women in particular have benefited from.

The family will therefore continue to play an extremely important role for capitalism, both economically and ideologically. This will inevitably result in constant tensions and conflict between the role of the family as a capitalist institution and as a site of people's personal relations – leading to contradictions and zigzags in policy and ideology.

Those contradictions can be seen with regard to domestic violence. The 'New Right' idea that men should have more control and authority over women within the family clearly conflicts with changing social attitudes. In the past, domestic violence was either sanctioned and legitimised by the state or, at the very least, viewed as a 'private issue' in which the state should not interfere. As a result of campaigns by women and the wider labour movement domestic violence is now considered in most countries to be a social problem and a crime which should not be tolerated.

However, while governments have changed laws and pledged to tackle domestic violence their economic agenda of cuts in benefits and services has actually made the situation more difficult. It is a positive step forward if women are aware that the violence is not their fault and that they do not have to put up with it. But if funding for refuges is being slashed, if public housing is no longer available, if benefits are being cut to the bone, where do you go and how do you survive?

In Britain, in the early 1990's, there were attempts to cut public spending by deducting money from the benefits of lone parents who were receiving child support from ex-partners. In other words, in order to save money, the state attempted to recreate the traditional economic dependency of women on men, even when they were no longer in a relationship. This had serious consequences for women, with some men using child support as a means of reasserting control over their former partners, including through the use of violence.

The limits of reaction

As economic crisis deepens, these contradictions become more acute. Right-wing governments can come to power, with a programme that includes reactionary policies against women's rights. The high level of abstentionism in elections due to the alienation of large sections of the electorate, in particular the working class – which in most countries now has no mass political voice – means that it is possible for parties to come to power with a relatively narrow social base. A layer of working-class men who have lost their jobs in manufacturing industry and have been unable to find an alternative or are stuck in low-paid, low-status jobs could be especially susceptible to reactionary ideology regarding women.

While many working-class women have been able to take advantage of economic and social changes to positively challenge backward ideas about their role in society, many men have seen their traditional role as 'economic provider' undermined, with no alternative role on offer. This can be emotionally and psychologically devastating for men who have been accustomed to identify 'masculinity' in this way – providing a fertile ground for prejudice if no unifying alternative exists. Because sexism and discrimination have become deeply rooted in society over thousands of years, a minority reservoir of support continues to exist for more backward ideas. This can be exploited by political parties to win an electoral base and can be drawn on by the ruling class in a time of crisis to sow divisions amongst the working class.

However, it is one thing to be elected on a reactionary programme – putting that programme into practice is another question. The Christian Right in the US played a major role in getting George W. Bush elected twice to the White House where they expected him to vigorously pursue a moral 'counter-revolution' in return. His election certainly created an environment in which the anti-abortionists in partic-ular felt more confident to push for further restrictions on a woman's right to choose. States attempted to introduce and sometimes succeeded in passing legisla-tion placing yet more obstacles in the path of women seeking an abortion. As is always the case where reproductive rights come under attack, women who can afford to pay have no problem in terminating a pregnancy while poor, working-class women suffer the trauma and hardship of unwanted pregnancies or are even forced to resort to the backstreet butchers.

But despite this 'drip-drip' erosion of abortion rights and a shift to the reactionary right in the US Supreme Court, the Christian Right were disappointed with Bush's presidency. One wing of the Republicans understood that if the party went too far in pushing the moral agenda of the conservative Right they would risk a political backlash, especially amongst women. A majority of people in the US still believe that abortion should remain legal. In April 2004 one of the biggest demonstrations in US history took place in Washington DC when over one million people took to the streets against the undermining of abortion rights. Any attempt at a full-frontal assault on Roe versus Wade, the 1973 Supreme Court ruling which granted women a constitutional right to abortion, would potentially ignite mass protests. Movements around social issues can in turn act as a catalyst for much wider protests in which all the economic and social grievances of the working class coalesce, threatening the capitalists' economic agenda and even their class rule.

How far the ruling class can actually go in rolling back the economic and social gains which women have secured in the workplace, the home and society generally will crucially depend on the level of resistance by women and the working class as a whole. An essential component of this resistance will be a united working-class independent political alternative which as well as organising collective struggle around economic and social issues, exposes and challenges the ideological attacks, including those related to the family.

part two

strategies
for change

1 'Liberal' feminism

So what methods need to be employed in order to achieve women's liberation? Throughout the history of the struggle for women's rights, different analyses of the causes of women's oppression have given rise to differing strategies for change. In what is often referred to as the 'first wave of feminism', initiated by women from the middle class and the growing capitalist class in the mid-19th century, the main emphasis was placed on securing change through legal reform. They challenged the ruling ideology, backed up by law, which decreed that there should be separate spheres for men and women and that married women were the property of their husbands. They fought for the right to have control over their own earnings and property, to have custody of their children after divorce and for divorce to be made more accessible. They also campaigned for higher education and for the professions to be opened up to women and, of course, for the right to vote. In general, although some were sympathetic to the plight of working-class women, their main concern was achieving equal rights with men of their own class within the existing economic and social framework.

The idea that discrimination can be eliminated and that women can obtain equality through gradual, incremental reforms within the confines of capitalism has been a constant theme in the struggle for women's rights and continues to hold sway today. Equality can be achieved, it is argued, through promoting legislation which eliminates discrimination and ensures equal opportunities, through educating, raising awareness and challenging prejudice, and promoting women into positions of power and influence.

Women on top

Even after years of important legal and social gains for women it is certainly still the case today that the main levers of power and control in society are in the hands of men. Women still constitute a minority in most national parliaments and on the governing bodies of global institutions like the United Nations, International Monetary Fund and World Bank. Photo opportunities reveal a sea of men in uniform suits interspersed with just the occasional woman. In the boardrooms of the major international companies and financial institutions it is still men who predominate.

In such a male-dominated world it is hardly surprising that securing important positions for women has become a key demand of many of those who want to achieve equality. For some, this is because they view women's natures, whether biologically or socially constructed, as different from or superior to those of men. Women are considered less aggressive and less confrontational. If there were more women global leaders, it is claimed, there would be less war and violence in the world. For others, it is not women's nature that is the key but the fact that individual women will, they believe, act in the interest of their sex as a whole once they are in influential positions, in the same way that men appear to do today.

Where women have managed to achieve 'high office', however, this has not necessarily been the case. Notoriously, Margaret Thatcher was British Prime Minister from 1979 to 1990. In the 11 years that she held this post she presided over a vicious programme of neo-liberal attacks which had terrible repercussions for the working class in general and for millions of working-class women of her 'own sex' in particular. Public-sector jobs were slashed, nurseries and other services closed down and single parents vilified.

It is true that Thatcher was a particularly 'aggressive' and 'confrontational' politician who never claimed to be a promoter of women's rights. But it is not the individual nature of the person in power or their sex which is important – what matters is which class interests they represent. There are undoubtedly female chief executives and managers of companies who would consider themselves 'feminists'. But at the end of the day, private companies exist to make a profit and when those profits are threatened the capitalist 'market' compels them to take whatever measures are necessary, however ruthless, in order to survive. If that means sacking workers or driving down their wages and conditions they will attempt to do so, regardless of whether those workers are male or female.

Similarly, female capitalist politicians who are elected on a platform of defending women's rights are ultimately in government to defend the interests of the capitalist class. While they may introduce some legislative changes which favour women in general, in areas such as domestic violence for example, at the same time the capitalists demand from their political representatives economic and social policies which attack the jobs and services which working-class, and many middle-class women rely on. Real and lasting change for those women would only be possible if the capitalist system as a whole was challenged, which these capitalist feminist politicians are unprepared to do.

'Post'-feminism

In the 1990s a number of 'post-feminists' declared that equality for women was just around the corner. Women had gained a whole host of reforms which meant that there were no longer any legal obstacles holding them back. Girls were outperforming boys in school, women were breaking into the professions and increasingly assuming positions of power and authority. The main barrier to women's equality was not the economic and social system or the 'patriarchy' but the attitude of women themselves. For too long, they argued, feminism had portrayed women as 'victims'. In order to become 'empowered' women needed to shake off the mantle of 'victimhood' and grasp the new opportunities which were opening up for them.[1]

With their emphasis on individual self-improvement rather than collective struggle, these ideas mirrored those of the neo-liberal governments in Britain and the US in particular, which stressed the need for individuals to take more responsibility for their own actions and lives. The dominant ideology stressed that if women were not successful then it was because of their own individual inadequacies rather than those of the capitalist system. Women needed to change themselves rather than change society.

There was a limited attempt by some 'old feminists' to challenge the 'new feminist' ideas which were gaining ground, particularly in the media. In her book, *The Whole Woman*, Germaine Greer relentlessly catalogued the discrimination and oppression which women continue to suffer.[2] But hers was a one-sided analysis, with little acknowledgement of the enormous economic and social changes which had taken place since the women's liberation movement of the late 1960s and 1970s.

'Post-feminist' ideas are partly based on material reality. Women have achieved many gains in their struggle for equal rights and discrimination is formally prohibited in most advanced capitalist countries. Social attitudes towards the role of women in society have been transformed in a relatively short period of time, with most people now accepting, for example, that women should work outside the home. Relationships between men and women have not been immune to these changes and it is undoubtedly the case that a layer of women feel more 'empowered' both economically and sexually. Many women, especially those who are young and well educated, feel that they are just as good if not better than men. While they are often aware of the wider inequalities which still exist in society, they remain confident that they will succeed as individuals.

Some will. But for most working-class women, however determined they might be, the struggle for self-improvement is constantly restricted by the barrier of economic and material inequalities which are an integral part of capitalism. The working-class woman who cannot afford to pay for childcare usually has no choice but to reluctantly take a low status, low-paid, part-time job. The lone parent who wants to go to university to improve her 'life chances' is held back by cutbacks in student grants, hikes in tuition fees and crèche closures.

As the gap between rich and poor internationally has grown ever wider, a gulf has also opened up between those women who have managed to climb the economic ladder, if not to the top then at least towards the higher rungs, and those women who still remain near or at the bottom. But, of course, even those women who do manage to take advantage of economic and social changes to improve their own situation are still subject to the wider sexual and cultural oppression which all women face.

Socialist transformation

Underpinned by inequality, exploitation and oppression, capitalism is incapable of bringing about the liberation of women. While it is possible to fight for and win some improvements in women's' lives, the underlying crisis of the capitalist system means that those gains are limited and constantly under attack. Real liberation, therefore, cannot be achieved through a gradual, piecemeal transformation of the current system but requires a revolutionary change in the way that society is organised and structured. Because of the double oppression which they experience under capitalism, both as women and as workers, working-class women have a particular interest in changing society. But by eliminating all inequalities of wealth, power and authority socialism would lay the basis for the liberation of all women.

2 Socialism

In a socialist society the means of producing wealth would be transferred from the hands of an unelected elite, concerned only with making a profit, to the democratic control of ordinary working people. Society could then be planned to meet the needs of the majority, not just a privileged few, and the basis laid for eliminating poverty, inequality, violence, oppression and environmental destruction. Already existing technology and wealth could be used for the benefit of the whole of society, in an environmentally sustainable way, and new wealth and resources generated by eliminating the duplication and waste which exist under capitalism, and through rational planning.

Despite the trappings of democracy, under capitalism real decision-making about most of the main issues which affect our lives resides ultimately with the small minority who have economic and social control. Socialism, based on democratic public ownership of the main businesses and financial institutions, would enable working-class people to have genuine control over every aspect of their lives. Through democratically-elected committees in the workplaces and communities it would be possible to participate in the running of society at every level.[1]

Economic independence

Socialism would dramatically transform the lives of all women, and those of working-class women in particular. The ending of production for profit and its replacement with democratic collective planning would enable the freeing up of resources to ensure that everybody had a minimum income and a decent standard of living. This would guarantee economic independence for women, bringing an end to poverty, especially in old age, and allowing women real choice in personal relationships. A planned economy would invest in the provision of public services such as childcare, eldercare and facilities for the disabled, relieving many of the burdens which individual families, and women in particular, shoulder today. Under capitalism, women are constantly made to feel guilty – guilty if they want to stay at home and look after their children and are claiming state benefits, guilty if they leave their children in order to go out to work. The provision of good quality, flexible, childcare which benefits children as well as parents would remove that guilt and offer parents real choice.

Together with a drastic reduction in the number of hours that people work, women and men's lives would be transformed. More free time would be available for relationships, for leisure pursuits and for training and education, allowing women to reach their full potential in a way that is impossible for the majority under capitalism. It would also enable women to participate in the democratic decision making and running of society, whether in their workplace, local community or on a broader level.

Public services

In capitalist society, housing is a huge problem for so many working-class and young people. When relationships break down working-class women can face homelessness or a life in sub-standard accommodation. Working-class men's relationships with their children also often suffer because of the way in which the housing and benefit system is geared around the 'nuclear' family. Good quality, publicly-provided housing, flexibly responsive to the needs of ordinary people, would relieve the financial and other stresses which expensive or inadequate housing place on individuals and personal relationships. It would mean that when relationships come to an end, for whatever reason, neither women, children nor men would be disadvantaged. And once the nuclear family was divested of its economic and social functions, people would be free to form relationships and households however they choose, allowing the possibility of a variety of forms.

Under socialism, users would be able to participate democratically in the running of all public services. A democratically-planned and integrated transport system, for example, would take into account the needs of all users as well as the environment. Other services, which are currently in the hands of private businesses and often only accessible to the rich, could be publicly provided and available to everyone. High-quality public restaurants would enable everyone to eat out rather than prepare meals at home, if that was what they wanted. Similarly, many household chores could be collectively provided. This already happens to a certain extent under capitalism but it is mainly the wealthy who can afford cleaners, gardeners, interior decorators, etc. New technological developments could relieve the monotony and grind of many jobs, not just in the workplace but also in the home.

A real right to choose

A socialist health service would also have sufficient resources to harness scientific and technological developments for the benefit of everyone, as well as massively increasing investment in preventative care. While this would benefit women's health in general, it would also give real choice over when and whether to have children.

Although increased accessibility to contraception and abortion has contributed to enormous changes in women's lives in many countries, a 'women's right to choose' does not truly exist today. Contraception is not 100% safe, is not always accessible and often brings risks to women's health. In a socialist society, the companies which produce contraceptives would be taken into public ownership and integrated into the health system. By withdrawing the profit motive it would be possible to carry out research into safer contraception, both in terms of its ability to prevent pregnancy and its effect on women's health. Similarly, it would be possible to carry out proper research into other issues associated with reproduction, such as menstrual and menopausal problems, and consequently develop safe remedies.

Today, even in countries which have relatively liberal abortion laws on paper, a woman's right to abortion is threatened by economic cuts and by moral and religious objections. In Italy, for example, 70% of doctors in the national health service refuse to carry out abortions on the grounds of 'conscientious objection', often in order to keep their jobs under pressure from the Catholic Church (abortions in the private sector in Italy are illegal) .

In a socialist society, access to abortion as safe and early as possible would be available as a backup for any woman who needed it. However, with better contraception, with sex education removed from the moral and social constraints which still surround it under capitalism and with the economic changes in women's and men's lives, unwanted pregnancies would undoubtedly diminish significantly.

At the same time, women and men with fertility problems would no longer be denied the right to have children because of insufficient resources or moral objections. A planned economy would enable resources to be allocated towards developing technology to aid fertility and massively increasing spending on research into environmental and other causes of infertility.

Social attitudes

It is clear, even from such a brief outline, that, from an economic point of view, moving from the anarchy of the profit system to a democratically-planned socialist system would drastically improve the lives of all working-class people and women in particular. However, as Engels explained, changing the economic basis of society also impacts on social relations. Capitalism is organised around the private ownership of the means of production and motivated by profit and competition. It is a system based on exploitation and inequality. This is in turn reflected in social structures, in the values and culture of society and in personal relations.

Socialism, in contrast, would be based on collective ownership and democratic control of the economy. Exploitation, inequality and hierarchy would be replaced by cooperation and negotiation. This would inevitably impact on how people related to each other and influence social attitudes, as we have seen from the experience of early hunter-gatherer societies. In a society which did not rest on private property and hierarchies of wealth and power and where the family was no longer a social and ideological institution, the basis would be laid for the total elimination of violence against women. When women have real economic independence and the profit motive no longer reigns supreme, women's bodies will cease being reduced to commodities to buy and sell. How we look and how we behave, how we express our sexuality will no longer be constrained by capitalist double standards and moralising.

The material changes brought about by socialism would lay the foundation stones for the complete elimination of all forms of oppression. However, attitudes which have been shaped by class society over thousands of years will not disappear overnight merely because property relations have changed. Those born and raised under capitalism will have internalised images, ideas and norms of behaviour from birth. Ideas and attitudes which have become deeply embedded can endure long after the material basis for them has been removed. A conscious campaign would therefore have to be waged under socialism, through a democratically-controlled education system and media, etc., to challenge and change 'hangover' attitudes from capitalist society such as sexism, racism and homophobia.

The Russian revolutionary, Alexandra Kollontai, explored the link between economic and social change and sexuality and personal relations in her writings at the end of the 19th and beginning of the 20th centuries. For Kollontai, the 'personal was political' long before the second wave women's movement made the slogan famous. She wrote about the need for a "revolution in the human psyche". Transforming the economic basis of society alone would not be sufficient to eliminate women's oppression, she argued; a cultural and psychological revolution was also necessary. This was particularly true in Russia, an economically and social- ly backward and predominantly peasant country. However, even in advanced industrialised countries where social attitudes have undergone a transformation over a relatively short period of time, a 'cultural revolution' would also be required.

3 What happened in Russia?

A lexandra Kollontai was a member of the Bolsheviks, the party which in 1917 led a revolutionary mass movement of workers and peasants to overthrow capitalism and landlordism and introduced a workers' state in Russia. This was a momentous historic event which inspired working class people around the world, raising their confidence that an alternative to the horrors of capitalism existed and that a socialist transformation of society was possible.

The subsequent rise of a Stalinist bureaucracy undermined many of the gains that the revolution had achieved. It strengthened the argument of those who maintained that a socialist revolution is bound to degenerate, and of those who claimed that women's oppression and patriarchy would still continue to exist in a socialist society.

The collapse of the Soviet Union and Eastern European states at the end of the 1980s and beginning of the 1990s unleashed a further barrage of propaganda against socialism in favour of capitalism as the only viable and credible economic and social system.

Gains of the revolution

The real gains of the Russian Revolution for the working class as a whole, and for women in particular, have consequently became obscured or distorted out of all recognition. Yet women's liberation formed a key component of the Bolsheviks' programme and the revolution paved the way for radical reforms which went far beyond those achieved by women in the more economically-developed capitalist countries at that time.

Marriage, for example, became a mere civil procedure, while the right to divorce was granted on request by either partner. Legal, free abortions were available to all women who needed them and homosexuality was legalised. The principle of equal pay for equal work was introduced and legislation passed to protect women in the workplace. This included 16 weeks of paid maternity leave, the right for nursing mothers to work no more than four days a week and to have regular time off for breast-feeding.

However, important as these gains were, the Bolsheviks recognised that women's domestic burden within the family had to be lifted in order that they could become economically independent, form free and equitable personal relationships and play a full and equal role in society.

The 1919 Programme of the Communist Party (as the Bolsheviks renamed themselves) declared that "not confining itself to formal equality of women, the party strives to liberate them from the material burdens of obsolete household work by replacing it by communal houses, public eating places, central laundries, and nurseries, etc". Housework and childcare would not just be the individual, private responsibility of women within the family but would be socialised and provided publicly by the state.

Day nurseries, kindergartens, public laundries and restaurants were set up and free lunches introduced in schools. In 1920, 90% of the population of Petrograd, the most industrialised city in Russia at that time, were choosing to eat in communal restaurants.

Transforming attitudes

But the workers' government also had to take account of the existing consciousness of both men and women. Women constituted a significant proportion of the workforce (40% during the First World War) which increased their economic independence and influenced how they viewed their own position in society. Nevertheless, most women (and men) lived in the countryside where the peasant family was still structured on a patriarchal basis – with a male head of the family exerting power and control over his wife – and backward attitudes prevailed. Many peasant women opposed the idea of communal nurseries, terrified that the government wanted to take their children away from them. They were suspicious of anything which they thought would undermine the family and their role within it.

The 1919 Programme, therefore, also stated that "the party's task at the present moment is primarily work in the realm of ideas and education so as to destroy utterly all traces of the former inequality or prejudices". A conscious campaign was needed to change the backward and reactionary attitudes towards women which were deeply ingrained within society. This included a concerted effort to engage and involve women as active participants in building the new social order. Women had played an important role in carrying out the revolution itself. In fact, it was female workers who sparked the February 1917 Revolution when, on International Women's Day, thousands marched to the factories demanding peace and bread and the overthrow of autocracy. Now their self-activity was vital for transforming society and achieving their own liberation.

In 1919, a special women's department, the Zhenotdel, was established to conduct work amongst women. Women's 'commissions' were set up at every level in order to involve women in the party and in the construction of the new society. The Zhenotdel was involved in tackling issues such as childcare, housing, public health and prostitution. It organised delegate conferences of working-class and peasant women, seconded women to government departments and party work, and young working-class women enthusiastically and energetically participated in outreach work with women in the countryside and remote parts of the country.

As well as producing newspapers and journals, the Zhenotdel organised discussions, exhibitions and developed innovative methods to raise the consciousness of women, most of whom were illiterate. There were particular problems reaching Muslim women in Central Asia where female volunteers were sometimes physically attacked and even horrifically killed. Despite these extremely dangerous conditions, they continued to seek out women in these areas, meeting secretly in bathhouses, for example.

The revolution itself unleashed enormous creative forces which affected every aspect of people's lives, including sex and personal relationships. Young people in particular questioned existing personal arrangements, experimenting with new ways of living and relating to each other.

Limits to liberation

Despite the best intentions of the leaders of the Communist Party, their programme for socialist transformation and women's liberation was constrained by the cultural and material backwardness of Russia. This had been exacerbated by the war, which left the country in ruins, and then further reinforced by a brutal civil war and imperialist intervention aimed at overthrowing the new workers' state.

Kollontai acknowledged that the socialisation of 'women's work' could not be easily implemented in an underdeveloped country devastated by war and civil war. Between 1919 and 1920, seven and a half million Russians died from famine and epidemics alone. In 1920, production of manufactured goods in Russia was just 12.9% of its 1913 level.

So, for example, while many communal eating places were established in the capital, the number of facilities in the rest of the country varied greatly and was often non-existent. Frequently the food was of such bad quality that workers turned their backs on public dining rooms preferring to eat in their own homes, falling back on the family and the traditional division of labour between men and women.

These material conditions also undermined attempts at transforming personal relations. Following the introduction of the New Economic Policy (NEP) in 1921, which was viewed as a temporary measure to revive production by introducing some market measures into the planned economy, unemployment skyrocketed with women hit particularly hard. In 1923, women constituted 58% of the unemployed in Petrograd. Formally women had the right to divorce but unemployment and economic hardship meant that in reality most were denied any real choice, forced to remain in unhappy relationships through economic necessity.

Those involved in the Zhenotdel carried out extremely effective work in raising the consciousness of women, ensuring that their concerns were addressed by the party and the government, and encouraging women to participate in the government and running of society. But the functioning of the women's department was hindered by the civil war, by staff shortages and by the fact that women themselves were exhausted and burdened with work and family responsibilities.

Counter-revolution

The Bolsheviks had always argued that it would be impossible to build genuine socialism in a single country, particularly one as economically and culturally backward as Russia. The revolution would need to be extended internationally to the advanced capitalist countries like Britain and Germany. Any reforms that the workers' government managed to introduce were, therefore, not only in the interests of the Russian workers and peasants themselves but to set an example to the working classes internationally, and to encourage them to also organise for a revolutionary change in society.

While workers in many countries were inspired by events in Russia, and revolutionary movements broke out in Europe and elsewhere, unfortunately none were successful in overthrowing capitalism because of the weakness of their revolutionary leaderships. The defeat of these revolutions and Russia's subsequent international isolation reinforced the demoralisation which had already set in amongst a working class decimated, exhausted and weakened by war, starvation and long working hours.

Economic backwardness and international isolation laid the basis for the rolling back of workers' democracy and many of the gains of the revolution, together with the rise of a bureaucratic elite, concerned primarily with 'managing' society and maintaining its own privileged position. The state-owned planned economy remained in place but workers' control and management through the soviets were replaced by bureaucratic centralised command from above. The economy developed but at an enormous cost to the lives of workers and peasants and to the environment.

Women' gains undermined

The interests of workers, including women, became subordinated to those of the bureaucracy, with Stalin at its head. In 1928, fearing that strengthening pro-capitalist forces within Soviet society could threaten the continued rule of the bureaucracy, Stalin moved empirically to force through the industrialisation of the country and the collectivisation of land. As part of this process millions of women were coerced into the workforce. But this was against a background of a deliberate running down of communal facilities such as nurseries, dining rooms and laundries which went much further than economic constraints dictated. This was because it was in the interests of the Stalinist bureaucracy to re-establish and bolster the patriarchal family as an instrument of social control. Mirroring the hierarchical structure of the bureaucratic state, it became a place where young people in particular could be disciplined to accept the power and authority of those at the top of society. As a consequence, much legislation was orientated towards strengthening the family as an economic and social unit. This was reinforced by the need for a growing labour force, with the bureaucracy launching campaigns glorifying and extolling the joys of 'motherhood' and urging women to increase their birth rate.

Many of the legal gains which the revolution had granted women were now reversed. Access to divorce became more difficult and abortion was made illegal in most cases. By 1938-39, 12.7% of every 100,000 deaths amongst urban women were caused by illegal abortions.

In 1930 the Zhenotdel was formally abolished in a situation where the original aims of the revolution, including the full economic, political and sexual equality of women, were far from being realised.

Genuine socialism

Nevertheless, bureaucratic degeneration is not the inevitable outcome of a socialist revolution, as many capitalist commentators argue. Nor is it the case that women's oppression will always be with us, even under socialism. The rise of the Stalinist bureaucracy and its undermining of the gains of the revolution were rooted in the specific conditions which prevailed in Russia and internationally at that time.

Clearly, a democratic workers' government in a more economically advanced country today would not face the same economic and cultural problems that the Bolsheviks did after the 1917 revolution. However, although socialism will lay the basis for a transformation in economic and social relations, it will require the active participation of working-class women and men in the planning and running of society, as well as the transformation of ideas and attitudes. At the same time the threat from capitalism internationally would remain a real one, underlining the absolute necessity not just for workers' democracy but for the struggle for socialism to be an international one.

4 Class and identity

What role will women play in the struggle for socialism today? Socialists and Marxists believe that the working class is the only force capable of leading the struggle to fundamentally change society. This is not because of some kind of 'romantic' historical attachment to the idea of the working class but because of the role which it plays in the production process under capitalism. Capitalism is a system based on competition and production for profit. The surplus from which profit comes is derived from the unpaid labour of the working class through exploitation.

A constant battle is being waged between the owners of the means of production, the capitalist class, and the producers, the working-class, over this surplus, which is reflected in struggles in the workplaces over wages, working hours, speed-ups and working conditions, as well as those to extend and defend public services. Workers, therefore, have a collective interest in fighting against and ending the economic exploitation which they face under capitalism.

Other classes and groups such as small business owners and peasants also suffer from the economic injustices of the capitalist system and could be involved in the struggle to change society. However, their economic and social position and outlook is not the same as that of the working class. Through collectively withdrawing their labour, workers potentially have the power to bring the whole economy to a halt. It is because of the potential collective strength which they possess within the workplace and the potential impact of this more generally in society that they have the main role to play in overthrowing capitalism and building a new society.

Working-class unity

Of course, capitalism will constantly attempt to divide workers, on the basis of gender, race, sexual orientation, etc., and therefore undermine their ability to unite to change their immediate circumstances and society as a whole. The capitalists, for example, have attempted to use lower-paid women workers to undermine the wages and conditions of all workers. At times, male workers have themselves fallen into the 'divide and rule' trap, attempting to exclude women rather than organising to ensure that all workers have the same wages and conditions. We see the same thing happening with immigrant workers today in many countries.

Socialists and Marxists, therefore, campaign for the maximum unity of the working class in industrial and social struggles and for the building of independent workers' organisations, including political parties, which can aid the collective struggle of workers and raise their confidence and understanding of the role that they can play in changing society.

While we do not believe that women can achieve liberation or that the problems facing working-class people in general can be solved through gradually reforming capitalism, it is through the day-to-day struggles to improve their conditions and defend previous gains that workers can become more confident and conscious of the need to generalise those struggles and to transform the system as a whole.

A victory, in a campaign against cuts to a local women's refuge for example, could give confidence to those involved and to others that collective action can achieve results. Even if the campaign were defeated, involvement in struggle could raise questions about why a facility that was so important to women experiencing domestic violence was being cut back and about the priorities of a system which puts profit before women's health and safety.

However, for struggles to develop into a successful transformation of society as a whole, a party is needed with a programme which can link the immediate needs of workers to the broader struggle for revolutionary change as the Bolsheviks were able to do in Russia.

Working-class women

As women now constitute around half of the workforce in many developed industrialised countries (and a majority in some), they are likely to play a crucial role in the struggle to change society. Even when they were in a small minority in the workplace, working-class women waged heroic struggles to defend and extend their rights as workers. Often the issues which spurred them into action were those which also affected working-class men: low pay, long hours, unsafe working conditions, etc. But inevitably, working-class women have also taken up issues of specific concern to them as women as well as workers, both in the workplace and more broadly in society. Although the struggle by women for the vote in the 19th century in Britain, for example, was initiated by middle and upper-class women, it also involved women workers who for many years remained 'hidden from history'. Very little was published about the female textile workers who petitioned and campaigned in the mills of the north of England to obtain mass support for the vote. Textile workers like Selina Cooper enthusiastically took the question of women's suffrage into their own working-class organisations. Local cotton trade unions agreed to ballot their members on the issue being made "a trade union question in the same way that Labour representation has been made a trade union question".[1]

Similarly, working-class women have waged determined campaigns for issues such as abortion and reproductive rights, sexual harassment, domestic violence and pornography to be taken up by workers' organisations.

Domestic violence

Sometimes, at first glance, it may not be clear how these issues relate to the workplace. Domestic violence, for example, as its name implies, has for many years been viewed as a private matter which takes place behind closed doors in the home. Nevertheless, female and male trade unionists involved in the Campaign Against Domestic Violence, which was initiated by Socialist Party (then Militant Labour) members in Britain at the beginning of the 1990s, campaigned for several years for domestic violence to be considered a workplace and trade union issue. Campaigning on this issue, which affects so many women, eventually resulted in every major trade union in Britain adopting a national policy on domestic violence.

Campaigners explained how women who are subject to violence and abuse will often have poor sick rates. After a beating they might take time off work for the bruising and swelling to disappear. But when they phone work they are unlikely to give the real reason for their absence, saying instead that they have 'the flu' or a 'stomach upset'. With more and more workplaces implementing draconian 'sickness monitoring' regimes, women experiencing domestic violence can face victimisation, including losing their jobs. Women workers may also need to be relocated in order to escape their abuser.

The training of workplace representatives in an understanding of domestic violence could encourage women workers to go to them for help. Campaigners explained that the trade unions, who still organise around seven million members in Britain, also had an important broader role to play in campaigning to raise awareness of domestic violence, to secure legal change and to fight for reforms such as more refuges, a decent minimum wage and childcare, which would increase the economic independence of women and their ability to leave a violent relationship.

'Cross-class' alliances

Because socialists and Marxists consider women's oppression a class issue, we have often been accused of ignoring the fact that all women are oppressed and not just women workers. This is a distortion of our analysis. When we refer to women's oppression as a 'class issue' we mean that it is rooted in and perpetuated by class-based societies and that a united struggle by the working class against capitalism is needed to lay the basis for its eradication.

Clearly, all women, regardless of class, are affected by issues such as reproductive rights, violence against women and sexism in general. For that reason, historically women have often come together across classes and in autonomous organisations to struggle against their shared oppression.

Some academic 'post-feminist' critiques associated with post-modernism have argued that, today, the differences between women are so great, that women have so many different identities based on class, race, sexual orientation, age, ability, lifestyle, etc., that it is no longer possible to talk of 'women' as a collective, social category and that, therefore, collective struggles by women are no longer relevant.

It is certainly the case that one of the weaknesses of many radical feminist theories, in addition to taking an 'ahistorical' view of women's oppression, has been the way in which they have treated both 'women' and 'men' as an undifferentiated group, ignoring or considering unimportant divisions based on class, ethnic group, etc.

Economic and social class can make a huge difference to how women experience oppression. Domestic violence, for example, takes place in every social class. The reasons why women stay in violent relationships are quite complex, involving physical, emotional, psychological and economic factors. However, if funding for refuges is not made available or if councils privatise social housing, it will be normally be working-class women who do not have the economic resources to live independently who will be particularly disadvantaged, perhaps being forced to remain in a violent relationship against their will.

Similarly, when abortion rights are restricted, wealthy women are usually able to travel to secure an abortion elsewhere, while poor women either have to carry on with an unwanted pregnancy or resort to illegal and often dangerous terminations.

Nevertheless, despite the existence of these very real and important differences, campaigns and struggles which involve women from all class backgrounds are likely to emerge as long as women's oppression continues to exist.

Where such campaigns and struggles have developed, however, they have experienced tensions and disagreements over ideology and what strategies should be employed to take the movement forward. The methods and aims of the female textile workers involved in the struggle for the vote, for example, contrasted with the middle-class leadership of the National Union of Women's Suffrage Societies

(NUWSS) with their emphasis on 'sex equality' and discreet parliamentary lobbying. Women "do not want their political power to enable them to boast that they are on equal terms with the men", explained Selina Cooper; "they want to use it for the same purpose as men, to get better conditions".[2]

As Sylvia Pankhurst outlined in *The Suffragette Movement*, the women from the East End of London who she was involved with wanted to end low pay and sweated labour; they were concerned with the plight of unmarried women, prostitutes and the welfare of mothers and babies; they saw the vote as a means of securing economic and social change which could transform their lives.

The danger of separatism

Historically, when working-class women have moved into struggle they have generally considered men of their class as their potential allies in the fight to defend their rights as workers and as women. And where movements develop today involving women from different classes and backgrounds, we would seek to orientate those movements towards the organisations of the working class, explaining the role that these organisations can play in taking individual struggles forward collectively, as well as in transforming society and ending the oppression faced by all women.

Radical feminists, however, have often drawn the conclusion that women's movements should remain separate from all organisations involving men. In the Campaign Against Domestic Violence, for example, there were sharp disagreements between those who wanted to orientate the campaign towards the trade union movement and those who opposed such an orientation on the basis that the trade unions are dominated by men, and men are responsible for abusing women. The latter also argued against the presence of male trade unionists on demonstrations. If this separatist approach had gained a majority it would have seriously weakened and undermined the effectiveness of the campaign in the workplaces and more broadly.

It is not inevitable, however, that workers' organisations will understand the importance of campaigning on issues of specific concern to women and of adopting a programme and a strategy which reflects their needs. Often, working-class women have had to battle long and hard to break down prejudices and convince male workers (and even at times female workers) that the issues of specific concern to them are not 'secondary' or a 'diversion' from more important questions and that it is in the interests of all workers to take these issues seriously.

Where the workers' organisations fail to respond, there is a danger that separatist ideas can hold sway. This happened in the struggle for the vote in Britain. The militant Women's Social and Political Union (WSPU), more commonly known as the Suffragettes, originated as a pressure group within the Independent Labour Party and initially orientated towards the labour movement. Between 1910 and 1914 the

Liberal government was under siege from a wave of industrial unrest amongst miners, rail workers and dockers, which spread to other sections of workers, including unorganised women workers in the sweated industries. Civil war was looming in Ireland over Home Rule.

The movement for women's suffrage added fuel to a social ferment which potentially threatened not just the Liberal government but the capitalist system itself. In the words of the Russian revolutionary Leon Trotsky, "a shadow of revolution" was hanging over Britain. But gradually, partly as a consequence of the outlook of its middle-class leadership but also in response to the Labour Party's refusal to endorse women's suffrage, the WSPU gradually evolved away from the labour movement, just as the social crisis was intensifying.

Individual 'militancy' such as stone throwing and later arson and bombing became the principal forms of protest – a substitute for, rather than an auxiliary to, a genuine mass movement to enfranchise women. Eventually the WSPU moved in a separatist direction with one of its leaders, Christabel Pankhurst (sister of Sylvia), claiming that 75-80% of men were infected with gonorrhoea, and adopting the slogan 'votes for women and chastity for men'.

The women's movement

The 'second wave' women's movement which arose in Europe and the USA in the late 1960s and 1970s also developed against the backdrop of a radicalisation in society involving anti-Vietnam War protests, the struggle of blacks for civil rights, student movements, working-class struggles and revolutions in the colonial world.

The nature and scope of the women's movement varied from country to country. Active participation was greater in the USA than in Britain, for example, but because of the greater strength of labour movement organisations in Britain, including the existence of a workers' party, the Labour Party (albeit capitalist dominated at the top), there was a much closer convergence between the workers' and women's movement. As early as 1968, women sewing machinists at the Ford motor plant in Dagenham, East London, took strike action to secure equal pay grading with male skilled workers, sparking off a wave of struggles for equal pay. Battles such as these inspired other sections of women and, in turn, many working class women were influenced by the demands of the women's movement. The result was a big change in attitudes by women themselves and more broadly in society, and important legal changes such as the Equal Pay Act and Sex Discrimination Act.

In Italy, the women's movement was closely linked to the radical Left. There it became a mass force, arising out of, and dovetailing with, an almost insurrectionary movement of the working class. Women consequently made big gains such as the right to abortion. Even where the women's movement was smaller in terms of the number of activists involved, its ideas, particularly concerning the family, violence against women, and the right for women to have control over their own bodies, had a much wider influence in society.

Nevertheless, serious divisions emerged, resulting in the domination of radical feminism and a fragmentation of the movement at the end of the 1970s. Radical feminism was unable to provide a strategy which could develop a way forward for the majority of women. For some, the 'personal' ceased being 'political' with 'cultural feminists' emphasising the importance of feminine values, 'lifestyle choices' and separate women's 'cultural spheres'. Changing oneself became more important than changing society.

While a small minority of women may have been attracted to the idea of 'separate spheres', it was clearly not a viable way forward for the vast majority. Other radical feminists took jobs in the 'women's industry' in local and national government or in women's centres. While the work carried on in these areas was extremely important, especially in women's refuges and rape crisis centres, for example, the day-to-day struggle for incremental reforms and, increasingly, to defend what had been gained against counter-reforms, became separated from any broader struggle to change society.

In other words, by effectively accepting the limits of the capitalist system, radical feminism represented yet another strand of 'liberal feminism'. However, even though radical feminism has manifestly failed to offer a lasting solution to the problems that the majority of women face, this does not mean that these ideas will not be revived in the future. Given the male dominance that still exists at every level of society, the continuation of discrimination and sexism, and in particular the high incidence of violence and abuse against women by male perpetrators, the idea that men are to blame for women's oppression and that the main struggle is against men and the 'patriarchy' can still gain a certain echo, particularly if the workers' organisations fail to offer a viable alternative.

5 Ideological backlash

The collapse of the women's movement dealt a blow to the idea of collective struggle against discrimination and oppression. This was reinforced by the move to the right by the former mass workers' parties such as the Labour Party in Britain and their transformation into open capitalist parties in many countries. This rightward drift took place against the backdrop of the extended economic boom of the 1980s and was given added impetus following the collapse of the Stalinist regimes in Eastern Europe and the Soviet Union, and the subsequent ideological 'victory' internationally for the capitalist 'free market'.

The leaders of the trade unions were also infected by these developments, promoting 'partnership' and 'co-operation' with the bosses rather than strike action and collective struggle by workers to improve their lot. As we have already seen, these developments led to a rolling back of many of the gains in the workplaces and in the welfare state, which working-class women and men had achieved through struggle.

It could also be argued that this has been accompanied by a rolling back of consciousness towards women's oppression in general and a re-emergence and growing acceptance of images and behaviour which in the past would have been considered sexist and demeaning. However, this has been a complex and contra-dictory process which should not be viewed in a crude, one-sided way. Attitudes towards domestic violence, for example, have undergone a sea change, with most people accepting that it is a crime which should not be tolerated. Unfortunately, while more women than ever before understand that domestic violence is not a private problem which they have to put up with, cuts in public spending undermine their ability to escape violence and abuse.

The 'new' sexism

However, in many countries there has been a growth in what has been dubbed 'the new sexism', with the revival and widespread use of sex and women's bodies to advertise a whole range of products from chocolate to toiletries and cars. Pornography, which was once confined to the top shelf of newsagents, has become mainstream – repackaged as 'lads mags'. High Street lap-dancing clubs, described as the fastest growing sector of the 'entertainment and leisure industry', have replaced seedy backstreet strip joints and become 'respectable'. University students' unions unashamedly organise beauty contests and even female trade union organisers define prostitution as a 'lifestyle choice'.

In the past, the women's and labour movements campaigned with some success to raise awareness of how sexist imagery objectifies and undermines women. By portraying them as body parts rather than thinking whole beings, sexist images strengthen the idea that women are inferior, second-class citizens, thus serving to maintain material inequalities such as unequal and low pay. At the same time, women appear to be sexually available objects for men to control and enjoy which can reinforce sexist harassment and violence against women.

Those who challenge this 'new' or 'retro' sexism are often branded as prudes, as sexually uptight and lacking a sense of humour. 'It's different this time,' it is argued. Yes, in the past these things would have been sexist and devalued and objectified women. But now they are 'ironic', a 'bit of a laugh' which the 'girls' can join in because they are more empowered and free to display and enjoy their sexuality. So they can laugh at, and join in with, sexist jokes and behaviour, they can frequent lap-dancing clubs and learn to pole dance and they can produce and enjoy pornography without feeling degraded or demeaned.

There is clearly a positive aspect to women being able to freely express their sexuality, to wear what they want, to live their personal lives as they choose, free from the moral shackles and constraints which bound them in the past. But in a capitalist society where institutionalised inequality still exists and where everything, including sex, is reduced to a commodity for sale, this constitutes a very limited and distorted view of sexual 'liberation'.

It might well be true that a minority of individual, well-paid lap dancers feel empowered and that some women see nothing wrong with joining men in lap-dancing clubs but the dancing still promotes an image of women as objects for men to control. Even if pornographic magazines are edited by females and women themselves buy and get turned on by porn, individual women are still exploited and abused in its production and these images objectify women in general.

It is true that attitudes towards violence against women have in general improved but it is still the case that one woman in four will experience violence from a partner or ex-partner at some time in their lives and one in seven will be raped. Young women are especially vulnerable. Scratch the surface and it becomes clear how imbedded backward ideas still are. Surveys carried out amongst young men and women in Britain have worryingly revealed that a significant minority believe that it is sometimes OK for a man to hit a woman (if she had slept with another man for instance) and, alarmingly, an overwhelming majority believed that girls and women sometimes encourage violence and abuse by the way they dress. Sexist bullying and harassment in schools is widespread with young women routinely called 'slags', 'whores' and 'bitches'. Popular culture both reinforces and reflects this and other sexist attitudes and behaviour.

Campaigning against sexism

Because anti-sexism has increasingly become equated with anti-sex, a layer of young women in particular accept and even actively embrace the so-called 'raunch culture', and things which would have previously provoked protest and opposition. Others, while feeling uncomfortable, put up with sexism, either because they do not want to be considered prudes or lacking a sense of humour or, as is often the case, because they feel isolated and cannot see a way of fighting back. This has particularly been the case in non-unionised workplaces where women have been subjected to sexual harassment and feel they have no choice but to put up with it or lose their job.

Sexist imagery and behaviour do not just undermine and devalue women, they also undermine the ability of the working class to fight back because of the potential to create disunity between men and women. They should therefore be challenged by the trade unions and workers' organisations in the workplaces and in society generally. However, campaigns against sexism need to take account of the changes in consciousness which have taken place over recent years, carefully explaining why sexist imagery, comments and behaviour are unacceptable and taking an approach which recognises the class nature of capitalism.

There is a big difference, for example, between objecting to imagery because it is sexually explicit, as the moral right and family values brigade do, and challenging the use of women's bodies being used to sell products and make a profit. Collective campaigns can help to raise awareness of sexism and the way in which big business dominate and control society. A campaign, for example, to lobby a local council to oppose the granting of a licence for a lap-dancing club could highlight how these clubs serve to perpetuate backward attitudes and beliefs about women while at the same time make enormous profits for the giant 'entertainment' companies. This is a very different approach from the moral right who campaign to ban sexually explicit images and 'immoral' behaviour, and it is one that we have successfully employed internationally, with campaigns against sexism in schools, against 'lads' mags' and lap-dancing clubs, etc.

There is also a difference between workers collectively campaigning in a workplace to raise awareness and to remove sexist and demeaning images of women, and campaigning for the introduction of legislation to ban these images more widely in society. Censorship can have unintended consequences. Two radical anti-pornography feminists, Andrea Dworkin and Catherine McKinnon, campaigned for many years for a ban on material considered 'harmful to women'. In 1992, a version of the Dworkin/McKinnon definition of pornography was incorporated into the Canadian obscenity law. Within two and a half years over 50% of feminist bookstores had had material confiscated or detained at customs. The main targets were gay and lesbian literature. Books seized by Customs included *Weenie-Toons! Women Artists Mock Cocks* because of its alleged "degradation of the male penis".[1]

The sex 'industry'

Sex has been a commodity to buy and sell ever since the rise of class society, but it is under the capitalist market system that commodification is all pervasive, as the very words 'sex industry' and 'sex worker' testify. Sex sells, and selling sex is increasingly becoming acceptable and mainstream big business. So much so, that some jobs in the sex industry have been openly advertised in job centres and there have even been cases in some European countries of women being told to take such jobs or lose their unemployment benefit.

The sex industry itself spans a broad spectrum ranging from the brutal forced trafficking of women as sex slaves and violent pornography to lap dancing clubs and sex chat-lines. Clearly, the degree of exploitation varies between and within different sectors, but all exploit and oppress to some extent the individual women involved and all objectify women in general, reinforcing the unequal power relations which are at the root of violence and abuse.

The sex industry is underpinned by the terrible economic and social conditions which women suffer under capitalism; low pay, poverty, debt, etc., but also abuse – sexual, emotional and physical – all of which are factors in women becoming involved.

Only socialism could lay the basis for the complete eradication of the sex industry by eliminating poverty and the inequalities of power and wealth which exist in capitalist society. But what attitude should be taken to the industry and the women involved in it today? Should socialists and Marxists support the unionisation of sex workers, for example, or the legalisation of prostitution? Both of these are controversial issues which have come to the fore in the recent period.

Unionising sex 'workers'

As socialists and Marxists we oppose the sex industry and have been involved in successful campaigns to close down lap-dancing and strip clubs or to prevent clubs and pubs from obtaining a licence to be able to introduce this form of 'entertainment'. We also campaign for an 'exit route', including alternative training and employment for women involved in the industry; for a decent minimum wage to end poverty; for student grants and the abolition of tuition fees (many of those involved in the sex industry are students); for decent childcare; increased spending and investment in resources for women who have experienced abuse; more resources for drug rehabilitation (in many countries a majority of street prostitutes are drug users); for safe houses and refuges for women who have been trafficked and against the deportation of these women under asylum laws; and, most importantly, for the creation of mass workers' parties with a socialist programme for a fundamental transformation of society.

We oppose the sex industry, not the women who are involved in it. As long as the industry exists these women should be entitled to the maximum protection and harm reduction that it is possible to achieve. So, if sex workers want to become unionised we would support their right to do so in order to collectively struggle to reduce some of the exploitation which they face and to make some improvements, however minimal, in their working conditions.

To oppose unionisation would be tantamount to arguing that because these women sell their bodies or because their bodies are a commodity they do not have the right to a safer environment. This is a moral, not a Marxist approach. However, we would oppose those who argue that selling sex is a 'lifestyle choice', that the sex industry is the same as any other 'work' and that jobs should be freely advertised in job centres, for example. We want to eliminate the sex industry, not legitimise it, but we also believe that the women involved in the industry have the right to organise to minimise the exploitation they face.

Prostitution

We would take a similar approach with regards to the legalising of prostitution. In countries where prostitution is illegal, laws mostly end up criminalising and endangering the women involved, and do nothing to reduce prostitution itself. In Britain, for example, women have been routinely fined for soliciting for sex and consequently sell their bodies again to pay off the fine. Women are often reluctant to report violent crime and abuse for fear of being arrested or deported.

While obviously campaigning against the conditions which force women into prostitution, and for measures which would help them to find a way out, we would also support measures which reduce the violence, exploitation and repression which women involved in prostitution face, whether at the hands of the men who buy sex, the traffickers and pimps who control them, or the state which criminalises them. We would not, however, support legalisation, where prostitution becomes a 'normal profession', where women are forced into privately (or more rarely publicly) owned brothels and big business (or local authorities) become pimps making huge profits out of selling women's bodies, and exploitation and abuse are legitimised.

The beauty industry

In a system based on inequality, hierarchy and exploitation, in which the media, fashion, beauty, sex and leisure 'industries' are in the hands of big business, real control by ordinary women and men over what is produced is impossible. Big business will exploit whatever it can to make a profit and will constantly seek to create new markets for its products, latching onto already existing attitudes in society and in turn reinforcing and perpetuating them.

The multi-billion dollar beauty industry promotes and therefore strengthens the notion that the most important thing about women is how they look rather than what they think or do. Women are constantly bombarded with images of an 'ideal' which most could never attain. But they spend millions on make-up, skin and hair products, the diet industry, fashion, even cosmetic surgery, in the hope that if they become thinner, more attractive, have a 'better' body they will be happier, sexier and more successful in their personal and working lives.

Only a very small percentage of women say they feel happy with their body shape and girls as young as 11 feel that they are too fat and are on a diet. While it is too simplistic to say that media images of women are the cause of eating disorders such as anorexia and bulimia, they are certainly a contributory factor and can delay recovery. Increasingly, men have also become a target for the beauty, fashion and leisure industries, as the big corporations seek out and artificially create new markets to exploit.

Women's anxieties about how they look can undermine their self-esteem and self-worth. American author Susan Faludi wrote about a cultural 'backlash' against the growing confidence of women, an attempt to put women back 'in their box'. (2) But although it is true that we have witnessed a backlash against many of the economic and social gains which women have achieved, this should not be equated with a big business or 'patriarchal' cultural conspiracy to undermine women in order to keep them 'in their place'. Big business feeds off and maintains women's anxieties and securities with one aim in mind, the pursuit of profit. Any other consequences are secondary, even though they may have the effect of weakening a 'backlash' against their own system.

Rebuilding workers' organisations as strong vehicles of collective struggle will be essential in the fight against sexism whether 'new' or 'old'. But a vital component of that rebuilding process will be an understanding of how sexism and the cultural oppression of women are part of a wider ideological apparatus which helps to maintain the capitalist system in place, and how challenging them is not peripheral but central to the struggle for an end to all forms of inequality and oppression.

6 Moving in to struggle

Historically women have moved into struggle in many different ways and working-class women, because of the double oppression which they face, are potentially some of the most determined fighters. In the textile mills, for example, in the 19th century, super-exploited women workers joined together with male workers in the trade unions to fight for their rights. In some sectors, women were excluded from the trade unions by male workers who feared competition for their jobs and the depression of wages and conditions, or believed that a woman's place was in the home and not in the factory. Unable to join existing unions, female workers organised their own, while at the same time fighting for unity with men.

Even the most exploited and downtrodden women workers, those who were not organised in unions and were considered 'unorganisable' by the trade union bureaucracy, waged heroic struggles. It was the 'match girls' in the East End of London, for example, who 'sparked off' the massive wave of struggle known as 'new unionism' at the end of the 19th century in Britain, when tens of thousands of previously unorganised workers formed new, combative trade unions. These match workers toiled in the most horrendous conditions, working 11 hours a day for a pittance from which draconian fines were deducted for minor offences. Defying the pessimists, they took strike action and, with the help of socialists, won most of their demands, including the right to organise a trade union.

The period of the 'Great Unrest', from 1910-1911, also drew super-exploited women workers into action, especially in the East End and South London: " Jam and pickle workers, rag-pickers, biscuit makers, bottle-washers, tin-box makers, cocoa makers, distillery workers, all sweated factory workers...... came out on strike for wage increases...... and most were successful."[1]

Today, in the ex-colonial countries we see similar examples of women workers, often very young, bravely challenging the near slave-like conditions which capitalism forces them to toil and live in. In the 'advanced' industrialised countries as well, there have been significant strikes by super-oppressed workers such as the cleaners, mainly female and immigrant, in the USA, fighting for union organisation.

Resisting attacks

Historically, women have also moved into struggle in their 'traditional' role as mothers and carers in the home, and as consumers. Through the Women's Co-operative Guild in Britain, for example, at the end of the 19th and the beginning of the 20th centuries, they waged campaigns against the adulteration of food and for better care for mothers during pregnancy and childbirth. Although, in general, they did not challenge the historical division of labour between men and women in the home, they did fight for an alternative way of organising working-class lives through cooperative childcare, shopping, laundries, restaurants, etc. Most of the women involved in these struggles did not work outside the home but were nevertheless part of the labour movement, and campaigned around 'workplace' issues such as equal pay. Women's sexual health was also an important issue for them.

Today, women are often at the forefront of campaigns to defend community facilities against privatisation, cuts and closures. If a local hospital is faced with closure everyone suffers, but women can be particularly affected. They are often frequent users of health facilities because of giving birth to, and caring for, children, and many women are themselves employed in the public (and increasingly former public) sector. As economic crisis and its aftermath force governments to slash public spending, it is inevitable that women will play a crucial role in resisting these attacks. Education, childcare, housing, transport, local environment, welfare benefits – these are all areas in which women have battled, and will continue to do so in the future.

Sometimes women have mobilised as 'auxiliaries' to working-class men who have taken strike action. It was the vital role that women played in the 1984-85 miners' strike in Britain – organising soup kitchens, speaking at meetings, raising finance, picketing – which enabled the miners to hold out for so long. 'Miners' wives' and other working-class women have movingly explained how being involved in that struggle changed their lives. It opened up new horizons and gave them confidence; nothing in their lives would ever be the same again.

Today, because of their increased numerical strength in the workforce, working-class women are much more likely to move into action as workers in their own right. This is particularly true in the public sector where they are often in a majority and where nursery nurses, teachers and teaching assistants, local authority and health workers and many others have fought determined battles against cuts, privatisation and deteriorating working conditions. As governments unleash even more draconian attacks on public spending in order to reduce deficits and make workers pay for the economic crisis, women will be to the forefront of bitter battles in defence of jobs, wages and services.

Campaigning amongst women

As in the past, women will also mobilise around issues of special concern to them because of their gender, whether through the trade unions and workers' organisations or through specific and autonomous organisations and campaigns. Sometimes it has been as a consequence of struggle around issues such as low pay or fighting against cuts and privatisation that women workers have gained the confidence to raise, and campaign around, questions of specific concern to them, such as sexual harassment and reproductive rights. At other times it has been as a consequence of campaigning around gender issues that they have been spurred into a broader struggle for economic and social change. Involvement in campaigning on single issues, such as for democratic rights, to protect the environment or against racism or war, can also awaken awareness of both gender and wider social oppression. In fact, in recent years women, and in particular young women, have been extremely active in these kinds of single-issue campaigns.

In many countries attacks on abortion and reproductive rights have been a catalyst for women to get organised and fight back. Sometimes this has been in response to attempts by governments to restrict access to abortion or other services, through legislative change, sometimes to prevent cuts in health care and other facilities undermining reproductive rights, and also to counter an ideological offensive by reactionary and religious forces.

Socialists and Marxists fight for the right of all women to be able to choose when and whether to have children: the right to free access to contraception to prevent pregnancy, the right to free abortion as early and as safely as possible in order to end an unwanted pregnancy, the right to free treatment for all those who want children and have fertility problems and the right to a decent wage, childcare, housing and other services, so that nobody is prevented from having children due to economic factors.

In these and other campaigns, the challenge for socialists and Marxists is to explain how gender inequality and oppression is linked to the capitalist system itself, and to orientate these campaigns towards the force which potentially has the strength to win temporary and lasting gains for women – the organised working class. This we were able to successfully do with the Campaign Against Domestic Violence, explaining how domestic violence is a class issue in that it is rooted in the structures and ideology of class society and how the organised working class can play a key role in securing economic and other reforms, as well as in the wider struggle to change society.

In many countries in which the Committee for a Workers' International (CWI) – the international organisation to which the Socialist Party is affiliated – is active we have taken initiatives on this question, including a very successful campaign in Pakistan in very difficult conditions. Swedish CWI members were also involved in campaigning against 'honour killings' after the brutal death of a young Turkish woman at the hands of relatives. Because violence against women is so widespread in every country, it is likely to continue to be a major issue and one around which women will move into struggle.

Anti-sexist campaigns are also likely to develop and expand. The revival and 'normalisation' of sexist imagery has divided young women in particular. While some mistakenly take the view that it is not a problem, others have been spurred into action, especially in the universities, campaigning against sex-industry themed club nights, beauty contests, etc. In Sweden, in response to sexism in the schools, CWI members took the initiative in launching a very successful campaign called 'Don't call me a whore', which rapidly gained broad and active support amongst young women and young men. In India, we were active in opposing the way that the beauty industry promotes a particular view of women in the pursuit of profit.

A revival of collective struggle in the workplaces and more generally in society is likely to give a further impetus to these and other campaigns around issues of concern to women. At the same time, gender and social issues could themselves become the trigger for a more generalised movement.

Workers' organisations

It cannot be taken for granted, however, that trade unions and workers' organisations generally will automatically understand the necessity of acting on issues of concern to women. Working-class women have often had to struggle for their concerns to be recognised or to push their organisations beyond mere lip service into actively campaigning around their specific needs.

Recently there have been examples of workers' parties and organisations resisting the demand for free abortion. In Brazil, for example, members of the CWI were involved in an important struggle around this issue in the Party of Socialism and Liberty (P-SoL), where its most prominent spokesperson, a woman, opposed abortion and refused to campaign in elections on the platform of a woman's right to choose. Where workers' organisations have successfully campaigned on this issue, real victories have been possible. In Britain, for example, a mass mobilisation by the labour movement in 1979 helped defeat the Corrie bill which would have cut the upper time limit for abortions at that time from 28 to 20 weeks.

The biggest social gains for women have been won precisely at times of heightened radicalisation and a rising level of class struggle. Today, women have a crucial role to play in rebuilding and strengthening the trade unions and workers' parties and transforming them into organisations which are prepared to fight for the rights of all workers in the workplace and more widely in society.

Socialist women

Historically, however, women have faced many material and cultural barriers to becoming actively involved in workers' organisations. Their 'double burden' of paid and unpaid work has left them little time for active participation. Hannah Mitchell, a working-class woman involved in the suffrage movement in the north of England, complained that women were fighting for the vote "with one hand tied behind us".[2] Unfortunately, workers' organisations have not been immune from the prejudices which exist in society as a whole and sometimes women have faced blatant sexism and discrimination from male activists. It has often been through joint struggle that these prejudices have been broken down – such as in the miners' strike in Britain in the 1980s for example, when many miners saw their attitudes transformed due to the key involvement of women in the miners' support groups, and also because of the participation of gay and lesbian activists in supporting the strike.

Socialist women have often played a prominent role in fighting for the rights of working women and encouraging their involvement in struggle. Eleanor Marx, the youngest daughter of Karl Marx, helped to organise exploited women workers in the East End of London, and it was the German socialist, Clara Zetkin, a friend and comrade of one of the most prominent female revolutionaries, Rosa Luxemburg, who first proposed in 1910, at an international conference of socialist women, that an international working women's day should be celebrated every year. She had been inspired by the tens of thousands of women who had taken to the streets in the USA to fight for their rights. Over one million people actively participated in the first International Women's Day in 1911. One week later, more than 140 women workers were tragically burned to death in the 'Triangle Fire' in New York, horrifically highlighting how the capitalist pursuit of profit takes precedence over the health and safety of workers and why it was so important for working women to get organised and fight back.

In most countries, International Women's' Day has continued to be celebrated every year on 8 March. The Russian Revolution itself began on that day in 1917 when women rose up and demanded bread and peace. As the Russian revolutionary, Alexandra Kollontai, commented in 1920: "The 1917 Working Women's Day has become memorable in history. On this day the Russian women raised the torch of proletarian revolution and set the world on fire."

However, over the years the original militancy and meaning of this working women's day have become obscured, so much so that in many countries 8 March has come increasingly to resemble Mother's Day, when women are 'spoiled' for a whole day and given flowers. It will fall to the new generation of working women to retie the thread of history and transform 8 March once more into an international day of struggle for women's rights.

Positive discrimination

The important theoretical contribution which Alexandra Kollontai made to the question of women's oppression has already been mentioned. She also campaigned for the Bolshevik party to develop specific material aimed at working-class women and to fight for reforms which would directly benefit them. She advocated the establishment of a women's 'bureau', under the general direction and programme of the party, that could organise and supervise work amongst working women and facilitate their recruitment and integration into the party.

In many countries today workers are posed with the task of rebuilding the trade unions into a fighting force and creating workers' parties that are capable of developing a mass base. Women could potentially be at the forefront of this process but their involvement in the struggle to defend their rights and for a transformation of society does not automatically flow from their dual oppression. On the contrary, it is this very oppression which can often hold them back from full participation. It is still the case today that women are underrepresented in the trade union movement, for example, even in countries where they make up a majority of the union's membership.

This has led to calls for, and the implementation of, positive discrimination – quotas and reserved seats for women in the trade union structures – as a means of overcoming discrimination and advancing the position of women. A similar debate has also taken place in some new workers' parties and formations over how to achieve equal representation of women within these organisations and as candidates in elections.

Positive discrimination can appear a very attractive means of overcoming years of discrimination and improving the involvement of women in workers' organisations. However, there is always a danger that it can be viewed as an organisational shortcut to redressing the disadvantages which women face. As such it can fail in its objectives, be divisive and obscure the real reasons why women are underrepresented.

A programme for action

If positive discrimination is not accompanied by the involvement of women at rank-and-file level and by democratic accountability, it can also lead to the development of a female bureaucracy, interested only in maintaining its own privileged position and divorced from the real interests of working-class women.

The gender of a candidate does not necessarily ensure policies and a programme to improve the position of working-class women in society. A female election candidate for a workers' party who supported, for example, alliances with capitalist parties which were implementing neo-liberal cuts in public spending would clearly not further the interests of working-class women as a whole.

In workers' parties, organisational measures to enforce gender equality in the selection of election candidates could undermine rank-and-file democracy and, indeed, be used as an organisational means of defeating an alternative political point of view.

If an organisation has women in leading positions this can give confidence to other women and encourage their participation. However, the main reason why working-class women get involved in trade unions and political parties is not because there are women in leading positions but because they believe that those organisations are fighting for the interests of concern to them. They want trade unions which fight to defend jobs and working conditions, fight for a decent wage, and which have policies to challenge discrimination in all its forms. If the unions were to wage a determined struggle around these issues, backed up with militant strike action, it would be an important step to actively involving more working-class women. A trade union which fails to address these issues will not sufficiently succeed in involving women, regardless of whether they are equally represented in the structures or not.

Positive measures

However, it is important to recognise that despite huge social changes, working-class women still have the main responsibility for childcare and housework leaving many little time to participate in meetings and activities. Lone parents are particularly disadvantaged as they often have nobody with whom to share the burden.

It is extremely important, therefore, that workers' organisations develop positive policies and measures to help women overcome these obstacles, such as providing or paying for childcare where possible and organising meetings and activities at a convenient time for women themselves. A sensitive approach is needed to the problems women face. Organising transport, for example, to and from meetings and activities so that women have more time, but also to ensure their safety.

A constant campaign is also necessary within organisations to raise awareness of issues of concern to women and to create an atmosphere which is welcoming to them. Although unity between working-class men and women is vital in the struggle to change society and to end oppression, this should never be used as a reason for not tackling sexist behaviour. There should be a zero tolerance attitude to all forms of sexism and educational campaigns to change the outlook of members.

Self-organisation or separatism?

Ideology can also have a negative effect on working-class women themselves. While there are undoubtedly many women who have no problems in fully participating in workers' organisations there are many others who will be reluctant to be fully involved because they lack confidence in their own abilities or feel that activism and politics 'are not for them'. This could be overcome by a conscious approach to developing the confidence of women, including, for example, considering the way in which meetings are structured and organised and, if necessary, organising special meetings, courses, schools, etc.

Sometimes there are objections to the idea of special meetings or bodies for women on the grounds that they are themselves discriminatory by excluding men. However, the same could be argued about any bodies which bring together any group of workers who share an experience specific to them, whether it is because of their gender, their race, their sexuality, the fact that they are disabled or indeed because they are young or work in a particular sector.

It is also argued that such initiatives will lead to separatism. This is certainly a danger, although not an inevitable development. It is important that any discussions which take place at special meetings are then taken into the workers' organisations as a whole in order to involve all members in those discussions and to educate and raise awareness generally amongst male and female members, and to avoid women's issues becoming 'ghettoised' or marginalised. While special meetings, committees, 'commissions', etc., can provide important forums for discussing issues of concern to women, for drawing up a programme and for developing campaigning initiatives, they should in no way substitute or bypass the general democratic structures and decision-making of organisations as a whole.

Achieving liberation

In the economic and social conditions which exist under capitalism, an end to all exploitation and oppression is impossible without the active participation of working-class women in the struggle for a radical transformation of society. Because of the material and social conditions which working-class women face they will inevitably be forced into struggle around issues which affect their class in general, as well as around those which are of special concern to them as women.

Sometimes they will ally themselves with other women who have an interest in fighting against their shared oppression. But it will be through a united struggle with working-class men against capitalism and for a socialist society that real liberation can be achieved.

However, a successful transformation of society will only be possible with a conscious understanding of how and why women are oppressed and through positive action to ensure that women are able to play a full role in their own liberation and that of the working class as a whole.

Notes

Part One

1. Have women always been oppressed?
1. Dobash and Dobash, *Violence against Wives*
2. See also Chapter 4, The Family and Women's Oppression Today
3. This is particularly true of the first part of the book
4. See in particular Eleanor Burke Leacock, *Myths of Male Dominance*, Monthly Review Press and Eleanor Burke Leacock and Richard Lee, *Politics and History in Band Society*, Cambridge University Press 1989
5. See Susan Brownmiller, *Against Our Will*, Penguin 1975
6. See Steven Rose, RC Lewontin and Leon J Kamin, *Not in our Genes*, Penguin 1984
7. Leacock and Lee, *op. cit.*

2. The Role of the Family
1. Dobash and Dobash, *op. cit.*
2. The Roman Censor was the highest state dignity, responsible for controlling the morals and conduct of citizens. Dobash and Dobash, *op. cit.*
3. See Chapter 5, The Ideological Backlash
4. See also Chapter 4, The Family and Woman's Oppression Today

3. The Family under Capitalism
1. *The Origin of the Family Private Property and the State*
2. An imperialist war waged by Britain against what later became South Africa
3. Sarah Boston, *Women Workers and the Trade Unions*, Lawrence and Wishart, 1987

4. The Family and Women's Oppression Today
1. See in particular Naomi Wolf, *Fire with Fire*, Chatto and Windus, 1993
2. *The Origin of the Family, Private Property and the State*
3. See also Part Two, Chapter 2, Socialism

Part Two
1. 'Liberal' Feminism
1.   Naomi Wolf, *op. cit.*
2.   Doubleday, 1999

2. Socialism
1.   For more details see Hannah Sell, *Socialism in the 21st Century*, Socialist Publications.

3. Class and Identity
1.   Jill Liddington and Jill Norris, *One Hand Tied Behind Us*, Virago, 1978
2.   Jill Liddington, *The Life and Times of a Respectable Rebel*, Virago, 1984

4. Ideological Backlash
1.   Nadine Strossen, *Defending Pornography*, Abacus, 1995
2.   Susan Faludi, *Backlash*, Vintage, 1991

5. Moving into Struggle
1.   Sarah Boston, *op. cit.*
2.   Jill Liddington and Jill Norris, *op. cit.*

socialist books

All of the books listed below are available from Socialist Books. To order further copies of this publication or any from either the list or the many other publications published by Socialist Books contact us at:

Socialist Books, PO Box 24697, London E11 1YD
telephone: 020 8988 8789 or email: socialistbooks@socialistparty.org.uk
or online at the socialist books **website: www.socialistbooks.co.uk**

other titles available
from socialist books

● **Socialism and Left Unity** by Peter Taaffe.
Published September 2008.
128 pages paperback
A critique of the wrong methods used by both the Socialist Workers Party, in particular, and similar organisations and groupings on the left.
Price £6.00

● **A Civil War without Guns: 20 Years On:
The lessons of the 1984-85 Miners' Strike** by Ken Smith.
Published May 2004. New Edition November 2008.
128 pages paperback
A balance sheet of this important struggle.
Price £5.00

● **Marxism in Today's World: Answers on War, Capitalism and the Environment**
by Peter Taaffe
Published November 2006. 128 pages paperback
This book is the result of a discussion with Italian Marxist, Yurii Colombo, it tackles head on vital contemporary issues: war, including the Lebanese conflict, the future of Israel/Palestine, the environment, China and its future, economic prospects for world capitalism and many more controversial issues. This book provides an invaluable Marxist analysis.
Price £7.50

● 1926 General Strike: Workers Taste Power
by Peter Taaffe
Published May 2006. 192 pages paperback
Written to commemorate the eightieth anniversary of the 1926 General Strike in Britain and, more importantly, to draw the lessons from this movement.
Price £7.50

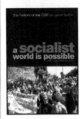

● A Socialist World is Possible: The History of the CWI
by Peter Taaffe
Published August 2004. 96 pages paperback
An account and celebration of the activity and contribution of the Committee for a Workers International (CWI) on the 30 Anniversary of its founding, showing how the role and influence of the organisation has developed and change -, in some regions of the world quite dramatically - from its humble origins.
Price £5.00

● France 1968: Month of Revolution -
Lessons of the General Strike
by Clare Doyle
Published April 2008. 96 pages paperback
First published in May 1988, Month of Revolution, looks at what caused this mighty explosion of workers' and students' anger and why it did not succeed in overturning capitalism. Clare argues that the French working class had power in its hands, that capitalism could have been abolished, and a truly representative socialist government brought to power. World history could have taken a very different course.
Price £7.50

● Socialism in the 21st Century:
The Way Forward for Anti-Capitalism by Hannah Sell.
Published August 2002. New Updated Edition February 2006.
96 pages paperback
An essential read for all anti-capitalists, trade union activists and socialists.
Price £5.00

- Pamphlet: **1917: The Year That Changed the World** by Peter Taaffe & Hannah Sell. Published November 2007, 48 pages paperback. Price £3.00

- **Planning Green Growth: A Socialist Contribution to the Debate on Environmental Sustainability** by Pete Dickenson. Published Jan 2003 (New Updated Edition, November 2007), 32 pages paperback. Price £3.00

- **Empire Defeated - Vietnam War: The Lessons for Today** by Peter Taaffe Published February 2004. 128 pages paperback
  A history of the Vietnam War drawing out the lessons to be learnt from this conflict, especially in the aftermath of the Iraq war. Price £6.00

- Pamphlet: **Join the Campaign for a New Workers' Party** by The Socialist Party Published February 2006. 36 pages paperback
  A brief explanation of why the Socialist Party has initiated the Campaign for a New Workers' Party. Price £1.00

- **Che Guevara: Symbol of Struggle** by Tony Saunois. Published September 2005. 96 pages paperback
  An appraisal of the life and role of Che Guevara as a revolutionary. Price £5.00

- **Cuba: Socialism and Democracy: Debates on the Revolution and Cuba Today** by Peter Taaffe. Published 2000. 128 pages paperback
  Defence of the Socialist Party's analysis of the Cuban revolution. Price £5.00

- **The Rise of Militant: Militant's 30 years** by Peter Taaffe. Published 1995. 570 pages paperback
  Story of Militant, forerunner of the Socialist Party (English and Welsh section of the CWI), from its birth. Price £10.99

- **Liverpool - A City that Dared to Fight** by Tony Mulhearn and Peter Taaffe. Published 1988, 500 pages paperback
  Militant led Liverpool city council's battle against the Thatcher government 1983-1997. Price £7.95

the socialist

weekly paper of the Socialist Party

Get your copy of **the socialist** delivered regularly by subscribing. There is a special introductory offer of 10 issues for only £6.00. Subscription rates:

- 12 issues: £9.00
- 6 months: £18.00
- 1 year: £36.00

You can telephone for either a direct debit form or pay by credit card on: **020 8988 8777**
the address to contact about subscriptions and international rates is: **Socialist Party - Subscriptions, PO Box 24697, London E11 1YD**

Subscribe online at: **www.socialistparty.org.uk/subscribe**

the socialist party

Socialist Party

join us

I would like to find out more about / join the Socialist Party ❑

Name

Address

Postcode

Tel No

Email

Trade Union (if applicable)

If you are interested in finding out more about the Socialist Party or our publications simply fill in this form and return to:
Socialist Party, PO Box 24697, London E11 1YD
email: join@socialistparty.org.uk tel: 020 8988 8767
website: www.socialistparty.org.uk

socialism today

theoretical journal of the Socialist Party

Get your copy of **Socialism Today** delivered to your doorstep.

Take out a subscription:
● One Year (10 issues)
Select your destination and price (includes post and packing)

www.socialismtoday.org

❏ Britain and Ireland - total price £18.00
❏ Europe - total price £20.00
❏ Outside Europe - total price £25.00

I enclose a cheque/ money order / travellers cheque
(made out to 'Socialism Today' for a one year subscription ❏

Name	
Delivery Address	
	Zip/Postcode
Country	Telephone
Email	

Cheques, money orders & travellers cheques, in sterling only, payable to Socialism Today
Credit card payments: phone 020 8988 8773 or fax 020 8988 8787
Send to: Socialism Today, PO Box 24697, London, E11 1YD

Contacting the Committee for a Workers' International

International Office CWI/CIT, PO Box 3688, London, Ell 1YE, Britain.
E: cwi@worldsoc.co.uk W: www.socialistworld.net
T: ++ 44 (0)20 8988 8760. F: ++ 44 (0)20 8988 8793.

If you want to contact the CWI in Argentina, Bolivia, Kashmir, Luxembourg, New Zealand, Trinidad or anywhere else ... then contact the CWI international office.

Australia: Socialist Party.
PO Box 1015, Collingwood, Victoria 3066.
phone: ++ 61 3 9639 9111
e mail: info@socialistpartyaustralia.org

Austria: Sozialistische Linkspartei.
Kaiserstrasse 14/11, A-1070 Wien.
phone: ++ 43 1 524 6310
e-mail: slp@slp.at

Belgium: Linkse Socialistische Partij/
Mouvement pour une Alternative Socialiste.
PB 131 Molenbeek Sainctelette.
phone: ++ 32 2 345 61 81
e-mail: ispmas@skynet.be

Brazil: Liberdade Socialismo e Revolução.
Caixa Postal 02009, CEP 01031-970,
Sao Paulo, SP
phone: ++ 55 11 9716 9960
e-mail: lsr@lsr-cit.org

Canada: Socialist Alternative.
903-633 Bay Street, Toronto,
Ontario MSG 2G4.
e mail: cwicanada@gmail.com

Chile: Socialismo Revolucionário.
phone: ++ 56 2 622 9004
e-mail: srcitchile@gmail.com

China: Chinaworker.
e-mail: cwi.china@gmail.com

Cyprus: Youth Against Nationalism.
Agias Elenis 36, Galaxias Centre,
ap.407, PO Box 1061, Nicosia.
e-mail: youthagainstnationalism@gmail.com
Czech Republic: Socialistická
alternativa, Budoucnost.
ul. V háji 4, 170 00 Praha 7 - Holešovice
e-mail: budoucnost@email.cz

England & Wales: Socialist Party.
PO Box 24697, London E11 1YD.
phone: ++ 44 20 8988 8777
e-mail: hq@socialistparty.org.uk

France: Gauche Révolutionnaire.
Les amis de l'Égalité, Centre 166,
82 rue Jeanne d' Arc, 76000 Rouen.
phone ++33 954 791 917
e mail: grcontact@hotmail.com

Germany: Sozialistische Alternative (SAV).
Littenstrasse 106/107, 10179 Berlin.
phone: ++ 49 30 2472 3802
e-mail: info@sav-online.de

Greece: Xekinima.
8 Gortynos Street, PO Box 11254, Athens.
phone/fax: ++ 30 210 228 3018
e-mail: xekinima@hotmail.com

Hong Kong:
YRHK, PO Box 72622, Kowloon Central
Post Office, Hong Kong.
e-mail: cwi.china@gmail.com

Iceland: Sósíalíska Réttlætisflokksins.
http://sosialisktrettlaeti.blogspot.com

India: New Socialist Alternative
(Dudiyora Horaata).
PO Box 1828, Bangalore 560018.
Phone: ++ 9180 2674 2616
e mail: newsocialist@dataone.in

Ireland North: Socialist Party.
13 Lombard Street, Belfast BT1 1RB,
Northern Ireland.
phone: ++ 44 2890 232962
e mail: socialistni@btconnect.com

Ireland South: Socialist Party.
141 Thomas Street, Dublin 8, Ireland.
phone/fax ++ 353 1 677 25 92
e-mail: info@socialistparty.net

Israel: Maavak Sozialisti/Nidal Eshteraki.
P.O. Box 5342, Tel Aviv-Jaffa 61053.
e mail: feedback@maavak.org.il

Italy: ControCorrente.
Via San Fruttuoso 50n 16143 Genova.
e-mail: info@controcorrentesinistraprc.org

Japan: Kokusai Rentai.
e mail: kokusairentai@hotmail.com

Lebanon: CWI Lebanon.
e-mail: cwi.lebanon@gmail.com

Malaysia: visit
http://asocialistmalaysia.blogspot.com

Netherlands: Offensief.
Postbus 11561, 1001 GN Amsterdam.
e mail: info@offensief.nl

Nigeria: Democratic Socialist Movement.
PO Box 2225, Agege, Lagos.
phone: ++ 234 805 304 5953
e-mail: dsmcentre@hotmail.com

Pakistan: Socialist Movement Pakistan.
phone: ++ 92 42 7288011
e-mail: revolutionary1917@yahoo.com

Poland: Grupa na rzecz Partii Robotniczej.
e-mail: ebsgpr@wp.pl

Portugal: Socialismo Revolucionario.
e mail: info@socialismo-revolucionario.org

Quebec: Mouvement pour le Parti Socialiste.
e mail: info@mpsquebec.org

Russia: CWI in Russia.
125167 Moscow a\Ya 37, Moscow, Russia.
e-mail: robert.cwi@gmail.com

Scotland: Socialist Party Scotland.
PO Box 10132, Dundee, DD2 9AR, Scotland
phone: ++ 44 7725119869
e-mail: info@socialistpartyscotland.org.uk

South Africa:
Democratic Socialist Movement.
P.O Box 596, Newtown 2193, Johannesburg.
phone: ++ 27 83 345 2017
e-mail: democraticsocialist@mweb.co.za

Spain: CWI Spain.
e-mail: info@mundosocialista.net

Sri Lanka: United Socialist Party.
phone: ++ 94 112 504647
e-mail: unitedsocialists@gmail.com

Sweden: Rättvisepartiet Socialisternas.
Box 73, 123 03 Farsta.
phone: ++ 46 8 605 9400
e-mail: rs@socialisterna.org

USA: Socialist Alternative.
PO Box 45343, Seattle, WA 98145.
phone: ++ 1 206 526 7185
e-mail: info@socialistalternative.org

Venezuela:
Collectivo Socialismo Revolucionario.
e-mail: socialismo.rev.venezuela@gmail.com